HEALTHY
made
SIMPLE

HEALTHY
made
SIMPLE

Delicious, Plant-Based Recipes
Ready in 30 Minutes or Less

Ella Mills

CONTENTS

08   Introduction

17   A few notes
before you start cooking

18   Prep-ahead breakfasts
& simple snacks

40   Speedy lunches

90   Midweek suppers

140   Cook once, eat twice

184   Index

189   Acknowledgements

190   About Ella

Prep-ahead breakfasts & simple snacks

21 Prep-ahead porridge

24 Prep-ahead energising smoothies

28 Prep-ahead toasts

30 Seedy green pesto muffins

33 Freezer chocolate chip cookies

34 Carrot cake flapjacks

37 Oaty almond butter and apple bars

38 Double chocolate oaty bites

Speedy lunches

42 Sweet and spicy kale, walnut and chickpea salad

45 Spicy tofu bowl with crunchy slaw

46 Chopped guacamole-style salad

49 Warm Mediterranean aubergine and basil orzo salad

50 Super green edamame salad

53 10-minute miso and ginger salad

54 Creamy tahini beans on toast

57 Harissa scrambled tofu on toast

58 Quick pan-fried tofu and herby yoghurt sandwich

61 Smashed chickpea guacamole sandwich

62 Crunchy satay potato salad

65 Creamy beetroot, lentil and yoghurt salad with toasted pitta

66 Avocado and butter lettuce salad with a crunchy protein topping

71 Mango, mint and chilli sunshine bowls

72 Herby summer rolls

77 My go-to green pasta

78 Miso mushroom bowls

81 Sun-dried tomato, basil and olive pasta salad

82 15-minute herby avocado noodles

85 15-minute black dhal

86 15-minute chickpea, edamame and miso stew

89 My every single day salad

Midweek suppers

93 Cavolo nero and walnut spaghetti

94 Slow-cooked courgette, olive oil and chilli linguine

97 Sweet potato and crispy lentil bowls with coriander and ginger yoghurt

98 Cosy roasted shallot and butter bean bowls

103 Garlicky broccoli and chilli protein bowls

104 Crunchy tofu, quinoa and tahini protein bowls

107 Creamy paneer-inspired tofu

108 Crispy one-tray hispi cabbage with garlic yoghurt

111 Herby jewelled rice with roasted aubergine, walnuts, mint and pomegranate

114 My everyday ginger and chilli stir-fry

117 Creamy beetroot, miso and tofu noodles

118 Comforting udon noodle bowls with mushroom and coconut

121 Crispy potato and paprika tray bake

122 Pan-fried sage and mushroom pasta

125 Lemony pea and broccoli pasta

126 Spicy black bean, quinoa and avocado bowls

129 Sticky miso aubergines with crunchy seeds

130 Crispy tofu goujons with pesto mash

133 Garlicky barley and green bean salad with herby almonds

134 Everyday veggie tray bake with mustard and cayenne pepper

136 Crispy cauliflower and thyme bake

139 Butter bean mash with garlicky almonds and greens

Cook once, eat twice

142 Everyday butter bean, carrot and sweet potato soup

145 Pea, broccoli and walnut soup with herby croutons

146 Nourishing lentil, mushroom and pesto soup

149 Chunky white bean and veggie soup with garlic croutons

152 My shortcut lentil bolognese

155 Simple tomato and basil orzo

156 Easy pea-sy curry

158 Spicy sun-dried tomato and aubergine ragù

160 One-pan spinach, leek and pesto orzo

163 Roasted cauliflower, fennel, tomato and Puy lentil tray bake

164 Creamy black bean, harissa and almond butter stew

167 Easy chickpea and veggie curry

168 Simple veggie and apricot tagine

171 Green bean, spinach and cashew curry

172 Speedy one-pot dhal

175 Roasted pepper, thyme and butter bean tray bake

176 One-pan peanut and cauliflower stew

179 Roasted Mediterranean veg and cannellini bean tomato sauce

180 Pesto quinoa fritters

183 Creamy leek, spinach and butter bean bowls

INTRODUCTION

Firstly, and most importantly, I want to say a huge thank you for buying this book, for joining our community and committing to nourishing yourself with healthy, plant-based deliciousness. I know there are thousands, if not hundreds of thousands, of resources to choose from and I really appreciate you choosing this cookbook as your healthy living guide.

When I sat down to write the first draft of *Healthy Made Simple*, I knew exactly what I wanted to do: to make eating well genuinely feel like a joy. I wanted to give you the tools you need to unlock a healthier life. I wanted to fill the book with vibrant, colourful, speedy recipes that would inspire and empower you, so that you'd be excited about creating new habits. In essence, it's a book dedicated to delicious flavours packed with goodness, and it will help you get healthy food on the table in less time, with less work and with fewer ingredients. That ease is what I need in my life, and I suspect it's what you might need too. I hope that what I share over the next few chapters will help you make meaningful changes in your life and that a few months from now you will feel very different from today.

FROM ME TO YOU

Before we get started, ask yourself a) how do you feel right now? and b) how would you like to feel a few weeks, months, or years from today? Would you like to move from frazzled, fatigued and overwhelmed to energised and a little less busy? If the answer to this last question is yes, as it always is for me, then I'm confident that leaning into these quick, nourishing recipes will make the world of difference. They will give you time to focus on other things, or even time to rest and recharge. I appreciate that you're probably juggling a huge number of commitments. I know I am. Between owning a fast-growing business and parenting two small children, I have very limited time. I've noticed the need to shift my habits towards simplicity over the last few years, which is why this book focuses on small changes and building simple habits. It's a lesson in making life easier for your future self.

Almost exactly nine years ago I sat down to write my first cookbook, a book that changed my life entirely, transforming my health, introducing me to my now husband (and business partner) and kickstarting our business. Back then I felt I'd discovered something that everyone needed to know: that vegetables tasted nice; plant-based eating could be delicious; healthy living was something we could all actually enjoy (previously I'd always thought it was more of a punishment); and eating a (predominantly) wholefood diet could fundamentally shift how we feel every day. A decade ago that was revolutionary, and the book went on to become the fastest-selling debut cookbook ever, as I, slightly inadvertently, opened the floodgates to a new conversation on health.

What I've learned, however, is that at times it was all more complicated than it needed to be. I wasn't nearly so busy back then, and every year that my life got busier, I realised I needed to shift gears slightly. When my first daughter, Skye, was born in 2019, I found my healthy habits slipping very quickly. I didn't have time for an hour of yoga, to soak my chickpeas all day, to spend all evening making dinner, to write long shopping lists and seek out niche ingredients. I'm sure you can all relate to that – whether it's prompted by changes in your family, career or just life in general, sometimes we all struggle. I had just a few minutes to spare (if that!) and I had to learn to use that time very wisely. It's taken me almost four years to master clever cooking – minimal ingredients, minimal fuss, maximum flavour. I'm now back in love with cooking and feeling better than ever. Healthy living fits into my lifestyle again, and I'm very grateful for that.

I know some of you might already be familiar with my story and why I wanted to revolutionise vegetables in the first place. There's a big part of me that feels uncomfortable going back through the history again (and again!). I can picture some loyal, long-term readers thinking, 'we know, you told us this before', so please skip this part if that's you! That being said, the reason I started Deliciously Ella is the very reason I care so deeply about what I do. It's why I write cookbooks, why I've spent a year writing and rewriting this book and why I want to empower you with the helpful tips and tricks I've discovered. I never want anyone else to feel how I felt then. In 2011, following my second year at university, I suddenly became very unwell, going from a normal student to effectively housebound in a matter of months. I spent the next few months in and out of hospital, having countless scans, tests and procedures. I had colonoscopies, endoscopies, cystoscopies, MRIs, ultrasounds, a hundred blood tests. I swallowed a camera, drank weird sugary solutions and woke up to Post-it notes saying 'nil by mouth' while I waited to be poked and prodded again. Eventually I was diagnosed with Postural Tachycardia Syndrome, alongside a few other syndromes. The condition affected the functioning of my autonomic nervous system. I struggled to control my heart rate and blood pressure, which meant that when I stood up my heart rate spiked at 150–180bpm (a normal heart rate is 60–100bpm), my blood pressure dropped, and I was so dizzy I felt that I couldn't move. It felt like my head wasn't connected to my body. I had chronic fatigue, brain fog, IBS, acid reflux, various other digestive issues, a host of infections, headaches, pain all over my body and a growing sense of both depression and anxiety. It was a chronic, relatively invisible illness that meant I spent most of the next year in bed or confined to my house, taking all sorts of drugs including steroids, antibiotics and antacids (peaking at 25 different drugs a day), none of which made a tangible difference.

I was only 21 at this point and it almost destroyed me; there were many moments where I couldn't see what my future could be. It unravelled everything I knew about myself and took me to absolute rock bottom. Rock bottom, however, changed my life. At that moment, I knew I couldn't continue along the trajectory I was on; I was going to give up or I was going to dig deeper than I thought I had the ability to do and find a solution. I chose the latter and began a period of research into what else could help me. This took me into the science of nutrition, looking at the latest research on how our lifestyles and our food choices impact our health. So, in May 2012 I changed my diet overnight, swapping my standard Western diet – lots of quick, convenience foods, not much fruit and veg – for a wholefood, plant-based diet.

Twelve years ago, the question of whether your diet could affect your health was not at all part of the mainstream conversation about health in this country, and I was met with a huge amount of scepticism. It also meant there was a lack of resources, and I couldn't find the healthy, delicious, plant-based recipes I wanted, so I set about creating them myself and Deliciously Ella was born. I was making it up as I went along back then, trying new recipes in my parents' kitchen and finding new ways to make simple foods taste great. I couldn't cook when I started, so I was very much jumping in at the deep end. If you're not a confident cook, then just know that if I can get the hang of it, so can you. I promise it's easier than you might think!

Learning to cook took time, and so did regaining my health. It was a slow journey initially, not an overnight fix. It often felt like two steps backwards, one step forwards, but I persevered in the knowledge that I had little to lose, and over the next few months and years my health stabilised. I started to feel like myself again, and I've been off my medication for over eight years. I never take my health for granted now. For me, good health is the cornerstone of a happy life. It allows me to be the person that I want to be, and I want you to feel the same way. Wanting us all to thrive is what pushes me to create these recipes, share tips on healthy living and drive forward our business. I want to make a nourishing life easy, something we can do day in, day out, for anyone who wants it.

It's not just me that's been through this transformation and felt the benefits. I read similar stories on social media every day. They're both incredibly humbling and deeply inspiring, and they show time and again that simple tools truly create meaningful change.

HEALTHY MADE SIMPLE

In the 12 years since I started Deliciously Ella, a plant-based or flexitarian approach to eating has become part of the mainstream, rather than a tiny niche. As the wellbeing industry has grown, so our collective knowledge of nutrition and its effects on our lifestyles has expanded too and there's an agreed consensus that healthy eating can positively impact our lives in so many ways.

The challenge lies, however, in implementing all this knowledge. How many times have you listened to a podcast, read a newspaper article, or watched a documentary about healthy eating and thought, 'yes, that's me, I could feel so much better too, I've got to change my diet', only to fall back into the same patterns a few days or weeks later? You're not alone. In fact, we did some research with YouGov last January that showed that while around half of us make New Year's resolutions linked to our health, only 6% of us continue those healthy habits past the end of January. If you relate to the feeling of wanting to make a change but not knowing where to start, or perhaps you've got out of the habit of prioritising your health, then don't worry, I've got you covered.

I'm not here to preach at you though. The world is awash with information on why we need to eat more wholefoods and more fruit and veg, and you probably know most of that 'why' already. If you don't, have a read of my last book – *How to Go Plant-Based* – it's got all the info. It would be remiss of me, however, if I didn't take a minute just to highlight the benefits. The reality is that what we eat impacts so much of how we feel, from our mood and our sense of self to our gut health, our energy levels, our sleep patterns, our immune system, our skin, our weight, our outlook, our patience and our risk of disease. Put simply, if you want to feel your best then you need to eat well, which by all accounts means following a predominantly (but not necessarily solely) wholefood, plant-rich diet. This means making healthy choices when it's easy and wherever possible, like on a Monday evening when you have no plans, or using those leftovers for an easy on-the-go lunch the next day. It doesn't mean not enjoying yourself and indulging on holiday or when you're out with friends. You must find your own balance, just as I've found mine, but generally to feel your best, the majority of what you eat should be fresh, vibrant and bursting with goodness: aim for 70:30 or 80:20, healthy to more indulgent food.

People often ask, is it really possible to change the way you feel by adopting new habits, like making quick healthy dinners in 15 minutes? Doesn't it have to be all-or-nothing? Don't I have to compromise? No, no it doesn't, and no you don't. That's the biggest myth in wellness. Small, achievable practices are proven to have long-lasting results, whereas huge changes and crash diets are proven to fail in 90–99% of cases.

So how do you keep that 70:30 or 80:20 up for the long run and move away from the crash diets? In my experience, you need two things: flavour and simplicity. Healthy must be easy and it must be delicious. That's how we unlock an enhanced sense of wellbeing, discover a genuine love of cooking, and make healthy eating a way of life, rather than a fad, and stick with it for decades, not days. We've got to learn to feel good, not guilty; joyful, not deprived.

It must be delicious, so that you look forward to sitting down and eating what you've made, rather than seeing mealtimes as one more chore, one more item on your to-do list (which is probably long enough already!). Meals need to be speedy and use simple, easy-to-get ingredients. You're probably already rushed off your feet, especially at the end of the day, hurrying back from work, uni or the school run (I'm always doing a mad dash finishing work and getting home to my two girls!), so you don't have time to run from shop to shop collecting niche ingredients. For me, a succinct shopping list is the only way to get a healthy dinner on the table.

I know everyone is different – our challenges all vary – but most of us are united in being busy and attempting to carve out time to exercise, manage our stress, cook healthy meals, get enough sleep and make time for friends, which can feel like a lot! I find it hard too, but I always feel worse when I let go of healthy habits, and the second I get back to what makes me feel good – especially preparing something quick and nourishing to eat – I feel so much better. Making time for your health is an act of self-care and knowing you're making time for it is empowering. I find that empowerment cascades into other healthy habits throughout the day and suddenly I feel like superwoman!

LET'S GET STARTED

In order to support the positive healthy habits, I've found that a few small tips and tricks, easy hacks, and prep-ahead recipes make life just that little bit easier: making simple breakfasts the night before; having a roster of almost-instant lunches up your sleeve and a list of speedy midweek meals (with ingredients that you can buy on the way home from work), cooking once to enable you to eat twice so that you have a delicious dinner as well as lunch sorted for the next day; are all game changers.

And that's what you'll find in the next four chapters: ways to make life easier for yourself today, and your future self tomorrow.

These recipes are designed for real life. They will help you on a Tuesday night after a long day of work. They will make stressful mornings less manic and save you time and money with your midweek lunches. It's not about Michelin-star recipes, it's about paring things back and focusing on what we all actually need to feel well nourished (and can feasibly achieve!).

So, each recipe has five simple promises:

1. It'll take *30 minutes or less*.

2. It'll contain *fewer than 10 ingredients* (I'm assuming that you already have olive oil, veg stock cubes, salt and pepper).

3. It'll have *no more than 5 steps*.

4. It'll be healthy and *packed with goodness*.

5. It'll be *delicious*: there's no point in it being easy and healthy if it doesn't taste good. I fundamentally believe flavour is essential or else you'll make one meal and then give up! For anything to be sustainable, it has to be enjoyable.

You don't need much to make the recipes either, no fancy gadgets or gizmos. All you need is a simple blender (you can make 80% of the recipes without one but it does help with textures and speed), a medium frying pan and a medium saucepan, a few baking trays, a steaming basket, and of course a chopping board and a sharp knife. The only other gadget that makes the world of difference is a mini professional chopper – I have one by the brand Ninja

(they cost around £25–30) as it'll save you a massive amount of prep time; depending on the recipe I reckon it often saves me a good 10 minutes.

Every chapter will equip you with the know-how and confidence to take charge of your health day after day. I believe in momentum and habit stacking, the idea that making one healthy choice ensures the next healthy decision is that little bit easier, that little bit more intuitive, and before you know it, you're in a positive cycle. Cooking nourishing food becomes a joy, and you'll have a spring in your step with all the extra time and energy these recipes will give you.

The other thing to have, is a relatively organised mindset – it sounds trite, but it really helps make cooking quick, calm and infinitely more enjoyable. Before you start, I'd recommend reading the recipe once or twice from top to bottom, so you know what needs to happen when and you can get everything prepped. Take a moment to assemble all the ingredients and tools that you'll need on your kitchen counter, so you're not running back and forth to the fridge and cupboards, which again will save you time and minimise stress. And finally pop a mixing bowl on the counter for your peelings and trimmings, so you can keep the surface clean as you go, which again helps foster a sense of calm. I like to put music on as I cook and flip it from feeling like a chore to a moment of quiet downtime, where I get to nourish myself (it helps when I'm doing it after the little ones are in bed!).

So, all that's really left to say is that I truly hope you enjoy the recipes and that they help you as much as they help me.

It's all about small changes, big results. Simple tools for a healthier life.

Let's get cooking!

Love,
Elle x

MY TWELVE TOP TIPS FOR A HEALTHIER LIFE

1 /START SLOWLY

We have a culture of all or nothing – we're often on or off a bandwagon when it comes to our food choices, but we know that diets don't work (90% or so of dieters regain all the weight they lost within a few years). Small changes that feel achievable are much more effective in the long term. Instead of setting yourself massive goals, think about gradual building blocks and lose the all-or-nothing mindset. Ask yourself, 'what one new healthy recipe could I try this week?' or 'what one simple swap could I make to nourish my body?'

2 /DON'T OVERCOMPLICATE THINGS

Healthy eating doesn't need to take hours or involve lots of unusual ingredients. One-pot meals or tray bake dinners are quick and easy solutions that require little effort or skill but are really satisfying. Likewise, don't get pulled in by clickbait headlines and contradictory advice: stick to simple wholefoods and getting lots of veggies in (most of the time). You likely don't need fancy gadgets, powders or gizmos!

3 /DON'T LET PERFECT BE THE ENEMY OF GOOD

To make healthy habits last, you need to fully accept that the path to feeling well won't be always straight or simple. Some days you'll jump out of bed, meditate, make a green smoothie and run to work before coming home and prepping a delicious dinner. Other days or weeks you won't do any of the above and you'll order a pizza instead. And that's ok. There's no such thing as perfect, no right way to do it, and certainly no dogmatic regime to follow. That said, don't give up altogether if you don't have time to cook all your meals or follow all the practices you would like to; small changes still add up over time. It's better to do something than nothing.

4 /GIVE YOURSELF CREDIT

It can be hard to make changes, to get up earlier, to carve out space for self-care, to make a healthy meal. We're quick to criticise ourselves for what we don't do, but try to celebrate your little wins and what you do do instead. You have to believe you can do it and that you're worth taking care of for your new habits to last in the long term.

5 /MAKE A (ROUGH) PLAN

It sounds simple but by loosely planning out your meals at the start of the week, you can shop for exactly what you need, saving you time, money and a whole lot of stress. It makes healthy eating much easier and more delicious.

6 /COOK ONCE, EAT TWICE

This is the best thing I've ever done for my health. The more you prep, the easier it is to keep eating well. Cooking double batches of your main meals, then portioning out the leftovers for later in the week, means you have quick, healthy meals whenever you need them. It's a great way to save money on midweek lunches too, and much more delicious than a store-bought sandwich. I almost never cook just one meal anymore; everything I make takes on a second life, even if it's just having extra dressings, grains or dips in the fridge.

7 /BALANCE YOUR MEALS

Combine complex carbohydrates, protein and healthy fats for optimal health. Eating these three food groups together helps to stabilise your blood sugar and improve both your mood and energy levels. Do you often find yourself having an afternoon slump at 4pm? Not combining these food groups might be why, so try adding all three to your meals and see what difference it makes.

8 /ADD PROTEIN TO YOUR MEALS

Protein keeps you fuller, reduces your hunger hormone (ghrelin) and reduces cravings, making it easier to stick to healthy eating. Add protein to every meal. For example, you can instantly turn a piece of avocado toast into a complete meal by adding a few pumpkin and hemp seeds and a drizzle of tahini on the top or mashing it with some white beans.

Here are the six best plant-based protein sources:

- Tofu, tempeh and edamame. Soy beans are a fantastic source of protein, as well as containing lots of other key vitamins and minerals, including calcium and iron.
- Lentils. Lentils are packed with both protein and fibre, are easy to cook and brilliantly versatile.
- Beans. You can use them in an array of dishes, as well as to make delicious dips, from a classic hummus to a red pepper and butter bean spread.
- Peas. They're often overlooked, but are an incredibly healthy, easy-to-use ingredient. Add them to a simple pesto pasta, blend them into a minty pea spread or mash into your guacamole for something a little different.
- Quinoa. It's quick to cook and a great swap for rice if you're wanting to add more protein to a recipe.
- Nuts, seeds and nut butters. As well as being packed with protein, nuts are high in fibre and healthy fat, so they're great at sustaining energy levels.

9 /EAT A RAINBOW

It's an easy way to think about healthy eating – are there lots of colours on your plate? Put simply, the more colourful foods you eat, the better. They're packed with antioxidants, vitamins and minerals that support good health. Vibrant red, orange and purple vegetables are especially beneficial, being packed with polyphenols, which help feed your gut bacteria.

10 /FEED YOUR GUT (AND EAT MORE FIBRE)

Studies show we should be aiming to eat 30+ different plant-based foods a week for optimal gut health, which is essential for good mental and physical health. Likewise, poor gut health is linked to a variety of chronic diseases, obesity and digestive problems. I know 30 might sound like a lot, but remember that herbs, beans, grains, nuts and seeds all count. The other benefit is you'll be upping your fibre intake, which is essential for a healthy digestive system, and stabilising your blood sugar, which means balanced mood and energy levels too. Most of us only get around 60% of the fibre we need, so including more plants in your diet will really help improve this.

Three easy ways to boost your fibre intake:

- Eat more complex carbs – starchy veggies, beans and whole grains.
- Include plants in every meal. Fibre is only found in plants, so you need lots of them – fruits, veggies, beans and legumes.
- Snack on nuts and seeds; they're easy to add into your day, they're delicious and they're packed with fibre.

11 /ENJOY IT!

Ultimately, for anything to be sustainable in the long run, it must be enjoyable, which means you need to embrace your wellness habits. Don't feel you have to do what you see someone on social media doing or follow one approach. Take inspiration from everyone and then do what works best for you. Only you know what you'll keep coming back to. Don't forget that a healthy, plant-rich diet is for life, not just for January. The benefits come from what we do on a daily(ish) basis, not from what we eat in one meal or on one holiday. So start small, think long-term and have fun experimenting with new flavours, colours and textures. Lose the preconception that — plant-based food is boring and get creative!

12 /STOP WAITING

Don't put off making changes because you can't make them all today. Stop waiting for the 'perfect time', saying 'when I lose weight, I'll do X or Y', or 'when I finish this project, I'll make time for myself', 'next week I'll make a healthy meal', because there will never be a perfect time. The best saying I've heard in a long time is 'the best time to plant a tree was 20 years ago, the second-best time is now.' Don't put off taking care of yourself – start today, start with one small change and watch the healthy habits stack up and your health improve!

A FEW NOTES BEFORE YOU START COOKING

Before you start, I wanted to share a few simple notes from my kitchen. These should explain anything that could be unclear and help make the recipes that little bit easier to follow.

1. Always read the recipe from start to finish before you start cooking, so you know what you need and what will happen when.

2. Take a moment to assemble and prep all the ingredients and tools that you'll need for a recipe on your kitchen counter, so you're not running back and forth to the fridge and cupboards, which will again save you time and minimise stress.

3. Keep a mixing bowl next to your chopping board for peelings and trimmings – it saves you time running backwards and forwards to and from the bin, and makes the kitchen feel calmer and tidier.

4. Equipment wise, I've used a blender (I use a Nutribullet), a mini chopper (I use the Ninja professional chopper as it saves me a lot of prep time), a steaming basket, a medium saucepan, a medium frying pan and a few baking trays.

5. Ingredient wise, I've assumed that you already have in the house olive oil, vegetable stock, salt and pepper. Each recipe then includes up to 10 additional ingredients.

6. When it comes to stock, I've mostly just specified a certain amount of hot stock, so you can use cubes, powder or homemade, whichever you prefer.

7. For salt, I use flaky sea salt and always have a box of Maldon sea salt flakes on my kitchen counter.

8. The prep-ahead breakfasts and simple snacks, speedy lunches and midweek suppers all serve two, the cook once, eat twice chapter recipes serves four so that you can make the recipe on one occasion and eat the leftovers on another occasion. All the recipes in that final chapter keep brilliantly, so you can save the second portion in the fridge for later in the week, or pop it in the freezer if you're not sure when you want to eat it.

CHAPTER 1

PREP-AHEAD BREAKFASTS & SIMPLE SNACKS

This chapter is about marrying wellness with deliciousness; helping you choose recipes that leave you feeling energised, satisfied and ready for a busy day. Your morning sets the tone for your day, so make it calmer, quicker and healthier. Just a few minutes of prep the night before can change your life.

Serves 2
Time 5 minutes the
night before

These are a daily staple in our house – they mean I can give my family a really nutritious breakfast with absolutely no fuss whatsoever. I would never put so many different ingredients into a porridge if I was making it first thing in the morning – there would just be too much mess when time is so tight. Either quickly heat the oats at home or take them on the go, popping them in the microwave at work or enjoying them just like overnight oats. All the goodness, none of the faff!

PREP-AHEAD PORRIDGE

WALNUT, CINNAMON AND APPLE

100g jumbo oats
500ml oat or almond milk, plus
   extra to serve
1 red apple, grated
large handful of toasted
   walnuts (about 50g),
   roughly chopped
big handful of raisins (about
   50g)
1 tablespoon almond or peanut
   butter
½ teaspoon ground cinnamon
1 teaspoon maple syrup
   (optional)
1 tablespoon shelled hemp
   seeds (optional)

CHOCOLATE ORANGE

100g jumbo oats
500ml oat or almond milk, plus
   extra to serve
grated zest and juice of
   1 orange
1 tablespoon cacao powder
1 tablespoon almond butter
pinch of sea salt
4 tablespoons milled flaxseed
handful of toasted hazelnuts
   (about 50g), roughly
   chopped
1 teaspoon maple syrup
   (optional)
1 tablespoon shelled hemp
   seeds (optional)

BLUEBERRY, BANANA AND PEANUT

100g jumbo oats
500ml oat or almond milk,
   plus extra to serve
150g frozen blueberries
1 ripe banana, mashed
1 tablespoon of peanut
   butter, crunchy or
   smooth
1 tablespoon chia seeds
1 teaspoon maple syrup
   (optional)
1 tablespoon hemp seeds
   (optional)

1. Simply stir the ingredients together in a bowl or jar, cover and leave in the fridge overnight.

2. The next morning, either enjoy cold as overnight oats or heat them up. To heat, you can either microwave, uncovered, on full power for 1–2 minutes, then stir well and add a little extra milk if needed. Or pop the porridge in a saucepan and warm on a medium heat until boiling, about 3 minutes, adding more milk if needed.

Serves 2
Time 5 minutes the night before

I know we all know how to make smoothies, but this prep-ahead method has changed my life. It's a simple swap: just spending five minutes on a Sunday evening quickly chopping and prepping freezer bags of ingredients means that all you need to do in the morning is chuck the contents of the bag in a blender with some milk and you're good to go. You can say goodbye to stressful, messy mornings when you have to quickly rummage through cupboards to find what you need and inevitably leave the house with the kitchen looking like a bomb-site!

PREP-AHEAD ENERGISING SMOOTHIES

BERRY, OATS AND PEANUT BUTTER

TO FREEZE
250g frozen berries
1 ripe banana
1 teaspoon ground cinnamon
2 tablespoons chia seeds
2 tablespoons peanut butter
50g porridge oats

TO BLEND
500ml plant milk

SUNSHINE MANGO SMOOTHIE

TO FREEZE
1 ripe mango
large handful of mint leaves
    (about 5g)
grated zest and juice of 1 lime
1 ripe banana
2 tablespoons shelled hemp
    seeds
½ teaspoon ground turmeric

TO BLEND
500ml coconut milk (from a
    carton)

SUPER GREEN SPINACH SMOOTHIE

TO FREEZE
1 ripe banana
1 green apple, cored
2 large handfuls of spinach
2 tablespoons almond butter
2 celery stalks
small chunk of ginger (about
    15g/2cm), peeled
2 tablespoons pumpkin seeds
2 tablespoons porridge oats

TO BLEND
500ml plant milk

1. Chop all the fruit/vegetables into bite-sized pieces. Put each set of ingredients, except the milk, into a freezer bag or Tupperware container and place in the freezer.

2. The next morning, tip the contents of your chosen bag or container into a high-speed blender with the milk and blitz until smooth.

Serves 2
Time 5 minutes

We all know how to make avocado toast but making something that's got added protein and fibre can sometimes feel a bit too much first thing in the morning. The last thing I want to do when I'm feeding my kids, getting them (and me) ready and out the door on time is make a big mess in the kitchen, leaving ingredients and washing up everywhere. Instead, I've started prepping most of my breakfasts the evening before; it's a game changer – more nutrition, more calm, more deliciousness.

PREP-AHEAD TOASTS

1 × 400g tin of butter beans,
   drained and rinsed
1 large ripe avocado, stoned
   and peeled
2 large handfuls of kale or
   spinach (about 100g)
1 tablespoon olive oil
grated zest and juice of
   1 lemon
sea salt and black pepper

TO SERVE
2 slices of sourdough toast
pumpkin seeds, basil pesto,
   sesame seeds or dukkah
   (all optional)

BUTTER BEANS, GREENS AND AVOCADO

1. Roughly mash the butter beans, avocado and a pinch of salt in a mixing bowl, using the back of a fork or a potato masher. A bit of texture is great, so you don't want it to be completely smooth.

2. Finely slice the greens (or quickly blitz them in a food processor), then tip them into the bowl of butter beans. Stir in the olive oil, lemon zest and juice, then season to taste with salt and pepper. Transfer to a jar or Tupperware container and leave in the fridge.

3. The next morning, spread the mixture on to hot toast and add any of your chosen toppings, if using.

250g frozen peas, defrosted
½ garlic clove, roughly
   chopped
juice of 1–2 limes
1 × 400g tin of cannellini
   beans, drained and rinsed
2 teaspoons tahini
1 tablespoon olive oil
sea salt and black pepper

TO SERVE
2 slices of sourdough toast

PEA, LIME AND TAHINI

1. Simply add all the ingredients to a food processor and blitz to a coarse paste. A bit of texture is great, so don't whizz until it's completely smooth. Season to taste with salt and pepper. Transfer to a jar or Tupperware container and leave in the fridge.

2. The next morning, spread on to hot toast.

1 tablespoon olive oil

300g mushrooms (I love a
    mixture of chestnut and
    wild mushrooms), sliced

3 garlic cloves, thinly sliced

½ × block of silken tofu (about
    150g)

1 tablespoon brown rice miso
    paste

1 teaspoon maple syrup

juice of ½ lime

pinch of cayenne pepper

sea salt and black pepper

TO SERVE

2 slices of sourdough toast

handful of chopped chives
    (optional)

MUSHROOM, MISO AND TOFU

1. Warm the olive oil in a large frying pan set over a
medium–high heat. Add the mushrooms and garlic and
cook for about 10 minutes, stirring often, until golden
all over.

2. Scoop the cooked mushrooms into a food processor,
then add the tofu, miso paste, maple syrup, lime juice and
cayenne pepper and blitz until smooth. Season to taste
with salt and pepper. Transfer to a jar or Tupperware
container and leave in the fridge.

3. The next morning, spread on to hot toast and scatter
over the chives, if using.

NOTE
The toast mixtures can be kept in an airtight container for up to
five days.

Serves 8–12
Time 40 minutes

If you want a speedy, savoury recipe that works brilliantly on the go and both as a breakfast option or a snack, these are what you need. They take less than five-minutes to prep and taste delicious on their own or cut in half and spread with mashed avocado or hummus.

2 large handfuls of spinach
    (about 100g)
bunch of basil (about 25g)
100g gram (chickpea) flour
100g porridge oats, plus extra
    to sprinkle
3 tablespoons basil pesto
150ml oat milk
100ml olive oil
1½ teaspoons baking powder
1½ tablespoons milled flaxseed
2 tablespoons pumpkin seeds,
    plus extra to sprinkle
2 tablespoons sunflower
    seeds, plus extra to sprinkle
flaky sea salt, to finish

SEEDY GREEN PESTO MUFFINS

1. Preheat the oven to 180°C fan and line a muffin tray with 12 silicone muffin cases (see note below).

2. Put the spinach and basil into a food processor and blitz for about 5 seconds, until finely chopped (but not puréed). Tip the blitzed greens into a large mixing bowl and add all the remaining ingredients with a pinch of salt. Stir until you have a thick batter.

3. Spoon the batter evenly into the muffin cases so that they're about three quarters full. Top with a sprinkling of oats, pumpkin seeds, sunflower seeds, and flaky sea salt and bake for 30 minutes or until a skewer inserted comes out clean. Leave to cool on a wire rack before eating.

NOTE
To prevent them from sticking to the cases, use silicone ones.

Makes 12
Time 20 minutes

I'm going to say these are life-changing. I have a really sweet tooth, but neither have the energy nor the need to make a big batch of cookies midweek. So I started making the dough on weekends, cooking half of it and then freezing the rest. Whenever I want something sweet I just pop a frozen ball of cookie dough in the oven and 10 minutes later I have a warm, homemade chocolate chip cookie.

2 tablespoons milled flaxseed

100g porridge oats

100g coconut sugar

200g crunchy peanut butter

4 tablespoons soy milk

½ teaspoon vanilla bean paste
    or extract

100g dark chocolate, roughly
    chopped

flaky sea salt

FREEZER CHOCOLATE CHIP COOKIES

1. Mix the flaxseed with 50ml of water in a small bowl and set aside for at least 10 minutes, until thickened. This will act as the binding agent.

2. Add the oats to a food processor and blitz very briefly, until they have mostly broken down but aren't completely powdered. Tip into a large bowl then add the coconut sugar and peanut butter. Stir together until evenly combined; you might find this easier to do with your hands, rubbing the ingredients between your fingertips until they resemble wet sand.

3. Next, add the soy milk, flaxseed mix, vanilla and chocolate and mix until just combined.

4. You can either bake the cookies now or freeze them to bake later. To freeze, line a Tupperware container with baking paper. Scoop out dessertspoonfuls of cookie dough into the Tupperware, using your finger to sweep them off the spoon.

5. Once you're ready to bake, preheat the oven to 180°C fan. Place the cookies on a shallow baking tray or baking sheet. Bake for 10–12 minutes, until crisp around the edges but soft in the middle. Leave to cool slightly on the tray then transfer to a wire rack and leave to cool completely. Sprinkle with a pinch of salt.

Makes 9
Time 30 minutes

Having a range of simple, no-fuss bakes to hand is so helpful. I like keeping something sweet in the house to snack on or give to my kids, so I cycle between the recipes in this chapter most Sundays.

150ml olive oil, plus extra to grease
150g coconut sugar
grated zest of 1 orange
2 carrots (about 125g), peeled and coarsely grated
1 teaspoon ground cinnamon or mixed spice
large handful of raisins (about 75g)
275g porridge oats
75g plain flour
sea salt

CARROT CAKE FLAPJACKS

1. Preheat the oven to 180°C fan and grease and line a 20cm square tin with oil and baking paper.

2. Put the olive oil, sugar and orange zest into a saucepan and bring to a simmer – don't worry if it splits slightly. Remove from the heat and add the carrots and stir to combine, then add the cinnamon, raisins, oats, flour and a pinch of salt and stir until coated.

3. Pour the mixture into the lined tin and press down with the back of a spoon until level.

4. Bake for 25 minutes, until golden brown. Leave to cool completely in the tin before lifting out and slicing into 9 squares.

'Adding the plain flour might sound strange but it's a miraculous ingredient here, ensuring the flapjacks don't crumble! We also tried rice flour and that works really well too, if you'd like to make it gluten free.'

These oaty bars are packed with goodness from grated apple, cinnamon, flaxseed and dried fruit, plus all the nuts and seeds. They're also incredibly simple to make, with just five minutes or so of prep time.

100ml olive oil, plus extra to grease
100ml maple syrup
100g smooth almond butter
225g porridge oats
50g flaked almonds
50g pumpkin seeds
75g dried fruit, roughly chopped (I love a mixture of dried apricots and cranberries)
1 tablespoon milled flaxseed
1 green apple, grated
1 teaspoon ground cinnamon
sea salt

OATY ALMOND BUTTER AND APPLE BARS

1. Preheat the oven to 180°C fan. Grease and line a 20cm square cake tin with baking paper.

2. Add the olive oil, maple syrup and almond butter to a saucepan set over a medium heat and stir until the almond butter has melted – this will take about 2–3 minutes.

3. Remove the pan from the heat and pour in the oats, almonds, pumpkin seeds, dried fruit, flaxseed, grated apple, cinnamon and a pinch of salt. Stir until combined.

4. Tip the oat mixture into the tin, pressing into the corners and flattening with the back of a spoon. Bake for 25 minutes, until golden brown, then leave to cool completely in the tin before lifting out and slicing into 12 bars.

Makes 9
Time 30 minutes

If you want something indulgent, super moreish and satisfying, yet easy to make, this is what you need. These double chocolate oaty bites with olive oil, hazelnuts and maple syrup are just delicious! If you've got a sweet tooth, bake a batch at the weekend and take a square with you to work; it'll make for the ideal 3pm snack!

125ml olive oil, plus extra to grease
125g coconut sugar
3 tablespoons maple syrup
2 tablespoons cacao powder
4 tablespoons water
350g porridge oats
100g dark chocolate, finely chopped
large handful of blanched, toasted hazelnuts (about 50g), finely chopped
flaky sea salt

DOUBLE CHOCOLATE OATY BITES

1. Preheat your oven to 180°C fan. Grease and line a 20cm square tin with oil and baking paper.

2. Put the olive oil, coconut sugar, maple syrup, cacao powder and water into a saucepan and bring to a simmer; don't worry if it splits slightly. Remove from the heat and pour in the porridge oats, three quarters of the chocolate and half the hazelnuts and a pinch of salt and stir until combined. Pour the mix into the lined tin and press down with the back of a spoon until level.

3. Sprinkle with the remaining chocolate and hazelnuts along with a pinch of salt. Bake for 20 minutes until golden brown. Leave to cool completely in the tin before lifting out and slicing into 9 squares.

CHAPTER 2

SPEEDY LUNCHES

Healthy eating shouldn't come at the expense of deliciousness, even when you only have a few minutes to spare. Every time I make one of these recipes I'm reminded of the power of 10 minutes – you don't always feel like making the effort, but every time you do, you realise what a massive difference it makes to feeling more energised. Discover colourful, quick recipes designed to help you thrive and boost your energy levels – be ready to say goodbye to that mid-afternoon slump!

Serves 2
Time 10 minutes

I love the contrast of the sweet, crunchy walnuts with the zesty lemon dressing in this recipe; it gives a lot of depth to something so simple. The salad is ready in under 10 minutes and uses just one small frying pan, making it the ideal midweek lunch. Plus walnuts, kale, chickpeas and avocado are all packed with goodness – healthy fats, proteins and complex carbs.

½ tablespoon olive oil

1 × 400g tin of chickpeas, drained and rinsed

large handful of walnuts (about 75g), roughly chopped to the same size as the chickpeas

¼ teaspoon cayenne pepper

2 teaspoons maple syrup

2 large handfuls of kale (about 100g), tough stalks removed, roughly chopped

1 ripe avocado, sliced

1 red chilli, finely chopped

sea salt and black pepper

1 lemon, cut into wedges, to serve

FOR THE DRESSING

grated zest and juice of 1 lemon

1 garlic clove, grated or crushed

1 tablespoon maple syrup

2 tablespoons olive oil

SWEET AND SPICY KALE, WALNUT AND CHICKPEA SALAD

1. Put the olive oil into a large frying pan over a high heat. Add the chickpeas and walnuts and fry for 3 minutes, tossing occasionally, until starting to turn golden.

2. Add the cayenne and maple syrup and fry for 3 minutes more, until the walnuts and chickpeas are coated in the sticky mixture.

3. Meanwhile, whisk the dressing ingredients together in a small bowl with a big pinch of salt. Put the kale into a serving bowl, pour over three quarters of the dressing and use your hands to massage the dressing into the kale – you want it to soften so that it's nice and tender.

4. Finally, tip the sticky chickpeas and walnuts on top of the kale and add the avocado slices. Drizzle over the remaining dressing, top with the sliced chilli and serve with lemon wedges on the side.

'To use up your veg, double the
slaw quantity, it'll stay fresh in
the fridge for about five days.'

Serves 2
Time 15 minutes

The harissa peanut dressing in this salad is one of my go-tos – you've got to try it. It packs a real punch and instantly turns simple ingredients into flavour bombs. The cucumber and coriander bring freshness to the salad, which brilliantly balances out the richness of the sauce, while the tofu ensures it's packed with protein.

½ tablespoon olive oil
1 × block of firm tofu (about 300g), cut into 2cm cubes
½ small red cabbage, shredded
½ small cucumber, cut into matchsticks
bunch of coriander (about 25g), roughly chopped, plus extra to serve
2 carrots, peeled and grated
sea salt and black pepper

FOR THE HARISSA PEANUT DRESSING
grated zest and juice of 1–2 limes
1 garlic clove, grated or crushed
1 tablespoon harissa
2 tablespoons soy sauce
2 tablespoons peanut butter (smooth or crunchy)
4 tablespoons olive oil

SPICY TOFU BOWL WITH CRUNCHY SLAW

1. Whisk the dressing ingredients together, starting with the zest and juice of just one of the limes and adding more if you want it even zingier. Then season to taste with salt and pepper.

2. Put the oil into a large frying pan over a high heat and add the tofu. Fry for 5 minutes, until crisp, then add in half the dressing, and fry for a further 3 minutes until the tofu is coated in a sticky sauce.

3. Meanwhile, make the slaw by mixing the cabbage, cucumber, coriander and carrot together in a bowl, then toss through the remaining dressing.

4. Serve the slaw topped with the tofu and an extra sprinkling of coriander and lime zest.

———

Make this a heartier meal by simply adding two servings of brown rice to the bowl, or pile the ingredients into a wrap.

Serves 2
Time 15 minutes

Essentially this is guacamole two ways, making it my dream meal. It's equal parts crunchy and creamy, and so far it's gone down a storm with everyone that has tried it. The dressing is pretty spicy but you can simply skip or halve the chilli to ease the heat level. The quick pickled onion gives the salad a lovely tang, while the tomatoes, lettuce and coriander add freshness.

juice of 2 limes
1 red onion, finely sliced
1 × 400g tin of black beans, drained and rinsed
bunch of coriander (about 25g), roughly chopped
100g cherry tomatoes, quartered
100g baby gem lettuce, finely sliced
½ avocado, sliced
½ red chilli, finely sliced
sea salt and black pepper
100g lightly salted tortilla chips, to serve

FOR THE SPICY AVOCADO DRESSING
½ avocado, roughly chopped
2 small garlic cloves or 1 large clove, roughly chopped
½ red chilli, deseeded and roughly chopped
3 tablespoons olive oil

CHOPPED GUACAMOLE-STYLE SALAD

1. Start by pickling the red onion. Put the lime juice and sliced onion into a small bowl with a pinch of salt and stir to combine. Set aside until needed, about 6–8 minutes, tossing occasionally so it pickles evenly.

2. Prep your veg while the onion is pickling, then put the black beans, half the coriander, the tomatoes, lettuce and avocado into a mixing bowl and give them a gentle toss.

3. Once the onion slices are nice and pink, scoop them out of the pickling liquid and add them to the salad bowl. Then pour the pickling liquid over the veg in the bowl.

4. Finally, make the dressing. Put the avocado, garlic, chilli, the remaining coriander, olive oil and 3 tablespoons of water into a blender and blitz until you have a smooth dressing, adding more water or olive oil if needed. Season to taste and pour the dressing over the salad, tossing it altogether.

5. Serve with the tortillas on the side.

MAKE IT A PACKED LUNCH
Keep the dressing separate – in a small jar – then toss everything together once you're ready to eat.

Serves 2
Time 15 minutes

This recipe pushes the 15–20 minute mark; essentially the length of time it takes will depend on how quickly you chop your veg (I'm pretty much bang on 15 minutes, but you may be a minute or so over or under that). It's worth that extra minute though as it's a great hearty lunch and my little ones love it too.

150g orzo

2 tablespoons olive oil, plus
    extra to serve

1 red pepper, finely diced
    (roughly 1cm cubes)

1 aubergine, finely diced
    (roughly 1cm cubes)

1 courgette, finely sliced into
    half moons

2 garlic cloves, grated or
    crushed

2 tablespoons maple syrup

3 tablespoons balsamic
    vinegar

grated zest and juice of
    1 lemon, plus extra zest to
    serve

2 tablespoons capers

bunch of basil (about 25g),
    finely chopped, plus extra
    leaves to serve

sea salt and black pepper

WARM MEDITERRANEAN AUBERGINE AND BASIL ORZO SALAD

1. Cook the orzo in boiling salted water according to the instructions on the pack. Drain, reserving a mug of the cooking liquid, and set aside.

2. Meanwhile, put the oil into a large frying pan over a medium heat and add the red pepper, aubergine, courgette and some salt and pepper and fry for 10 minutes, until softened. Tip in the garlic for the last 30 seconds or so, and cook until it smells fragrant.

3. Add the maple syrup, balsamic vinegar, lemon and capers to the pan along with 4 tablespoons of the pasta cooking liquid and simmer for 2 minutes to get a glossy sauce. Tip in the cooked orzo, stir to coat it in the sauce, then toss through the basil. Check the seasoning, adding more salt and pepper if needed.

4. Serve in bowls with an extra drizzle of oil, the basil leaves and extra lemon zest on top.

'Make sure you cut your veg nice and small, otherwise they won't cook fully.'

Serves 2
Time 15 minutes

I feel pretty good about my life when I eat this. It's packed with goodness, and you really feel that every bite is so nourishing, like you're doing something healthy for yourself, yet it's still so simple to make. On my timer it comes in at 13–14 minutes, basically as long as it takes to cook the quinoa.

100g quinoa
100g frozen edamame
large handful of spinach
    (about 50g), shredded
4 tablespoons pumpkin seeds
½ cucumber, diced
sea salt and black pepper
grated zest of 1 lemon, to
    serve (optional)

FOR THE DRESSING
bunch of coriander or flat-leaf
    parsley (about 25g)
large handful of spinach
    (about 50g)
2 tablespoons tahini
2 tablespoons maple
juice of ½–1 lemon (depending
    on preference)
4 tablespoons olive oil

SUPER GREEN EDAMAME SALAD

1. Cook the quinoa in salted water according to the instructions on the pack, adding the edamame to the pan for the last 2 minutes. Drain any liquid and set aside to cool slightly.

2. While the quinoa cooks, make the dressing. Simply put the dressing ingredients, plus 2 tablespoons of water into a blender and blitz until smooth, adding more water or olive oil if needed.

3. Toss the quinoa and edamame, spinach, pumpkin seeds and cucumber in a bowl with the dressing. Then grate a little lemon zest over the top to serve, if you like.

MAKE IT A PACKED LUNCH
This is a perfect on-the-go recipe. Simply leave the quinoa to cool then follow the same instructions and pop the tossed salad into an airtight container.

'If you don't have a
blender you can still make
the dressing. Simply add
all of the spinach to the
salad, then finely chop your
chosen herb and whisk
it together with the other
dressing ingredients.'

'To peel your ginger quickly
and easily, use the back of a
teaspoon – it works a charm!'

Serves 2
Time 10 minutes

The recipe couldn't be easier – it's the teriyaki dressing that brings it to life. I love a good dressing; it's what makes a meal for me, so I've been pretty heavy-handed here. You could always start with half the amount and then slowly add the rest, if you like it less punchy.

1 × 400g tin of black beans, drained and rinsed

100g frozen edamame beans

2 carrots, peeled and cut into thin matchsticks (or grated)

½ cucumber, finely sliced into thin matchsticks or batons

1 red pepper, finely sliced into thin matchsticks

1 red chilli, finely sliced

FOR THE TERIYAKI
DRESSING

small chunk of ginger, (about 50g/5cm) peeled and grated

3 tablespoons rice wine vinegar

2 tablespoons maple syrup

1½ tablespoons brown rice miso paste

3 tablespoons olive oil

1 red chilli, finely chopped

10-MINUTE MISO AND GINGER SALAD

1. Start by simply whisking the dressing ingredients together in a small bowl.

2. Next, put the black beans and edamame beans into a frying pan over a high heat. Add half the dressing and fry for 3–4 minutes, until the beans have softened and are coated in a sticky sauce. Set aside to cool for a minute or two.

3. Place the carrots, cucumber, pepper and bean mixture into sections in a bowl. Drizzle over the remaining dressing and sprinkle over the chilli to finish.

MAKE IT A PACKED LUNCH
If you're really tight on time, simply skip the cooking step. Use the drained black beans straight from the can and just blanch the edamame, popping them into a bowl, covering with boiling water for two minutes, then draining.

Serves 2
Time 15 minutes

Extra creamy, brilliantly tangy, these are a modern twist on classic beans on toast. They take about 10 minutes to make and one minute to eat. They're really filling, perfect for hungry, working from home days (or a speedy supper on a long day).

1 tablespoon olive oil, plus extra to finish
1 × 400g tin of butter beans, drained and rinsed
2 large garlic cloves, 1 peeled and crushed or grated, 1 peeled and left whole
2 thick slices of sourdough
handful of salad leaves
sea salt and black pepper

FOR THE SAUCE
1 tablespoon tahini
juice of 1 lemon, plus the grated zest to serve
1 heaped teaspoon Dijon mustard
3 tablespoons capers (1 tablespoon whole, 2 tablespoons very finely chopped)
2 tablespoons nutritional yeast
2 tablespoons olive oil
1–2 teaspoons maple syrup
5 tablespoons water

MAKE IT DINNER
You could serve these beans in a baked sweet potato with a side salad topped with lemon zest and a handful of chives, if you want them to be a little fancier.

CREAMY TAHINI BEANS ON TOAST

1. Place a medium frying pan over a medium heat and add the olive oil. Once warm, add the butter beans and a pinch of salt. Let them cook for 5 minutes, stirring every now and again.

2. While the beans cook, make the sauce by whisking all the ingredients together in a small bowl. You'll need to make sure you cut the chopped capers really finely so that they melt into the rest of the mix.

3. Add the crushed garlic to the butter beans about 30 seconds before the 5 minutes is up and cook until fragrant, then pour in three quarters of the dressing. Stir well and let it all cook together for a minute or so, until the beans are coated in a nice glossy sauce, which has reduced slightly. I get my sourdough toasting at this point.

4. Drizzle a little olive oil on to the toast and rub it with the whole garlic clove. Toss the salad leaves with the remaining dressing.

5. Pile the hot, creamy beans on top of the toast, adding a drizzle of oil and lots of salt and pepper and lemon zest to finish. Serve immediately (it's not anywhere near as delicious otherwise).

'Swap tahini for plant-based (or regular) mayo; Greek-style yoghurt also works well.'

'Make sure the onion really
is finely chopped, or else it
won't cook in 5 minutes and
the dish will taste of raw
onion. A small chopper (I have
a Ninja) saves you a huge
amount of time with this.'

If I want a protein-packed lunch in minutes, this is my go-to. It's delicious, very easy to make and has about 20g of plant protein in each serving. Served with sourdough and avocado, it's a brilliantly balanced meal that'll give you loads of long-lasting energy.

½ tablespoon olive oil

1 small red onion, finely chopped

2 garlic cloves, crushed

1 tablespoon harissa

pinch of ground turmeric (optional)

1 teaspoon maple syrup

1 × block of silken or firm tofu (about 300g), drained (see Note below)

large handful of spinach (about 50g), finely chopped

sea salt

TO SERVE

2 thick slices of sourdough

1 ripe avocado, finely sliced

lemon wedges

HARISSA SCRAMBLED TOFU ON TOAST

1. Heat the olive oil in a large pan over a medium heat. Once warm, add the onion, garlic and a pinch of salt, cook for 5 minutes, until soft.

2. Once soft, add the harissa, turmeric (if using) and maple syrup and stir to combine. Using your hands, crumble in the tofu and stir through.

3. Cook the scramble for another 5 minutes, until the tofu is hot, stirring every now and again. Add the spinach for the last 30 seconds or so, letting it wilt slightly (you don't want it totally wilted or else you won't have the texture contrast). I put my sourdough on to toast at this point.

4. To serve, layer the avocado and tofu on the slices of toast, adding a lemon wedge on the side.

NOTE
Both styles of tofu work well, the silken is a little smoother, making the finish more velvety, the firmer tofu is a little chunkier and heartier.

Serves 2
Time 15 minutes

With around 20g protein per sandwich, this is a brilliant lunch idea that will keep you satisfied and full of energy all afternoon. The yoghurt is fresh and zingy, with a lovely kick from the chilli; the tofu is chunky and a little crispy and the quick pickled cucumber adds a great tang. It may not sound like a showstopper, but trust me, it really is, and has become a (slightly unexpected) hit in our house.

2 tablespoons apple cider
   vinegar
1 teaspoon maple syrup
½ cucumber, peeled into
   ribbons
grated zest of 1 lemon
1 tablespoon olive oil, plus
   extra to drizzle
1 × block of firm tofu (about
   300g), cut lengthways into
   4 slices
2–4 slices of sourdough
   (depending on whether you
   want an open sandwich or
   not)
1 red chilli, finely chopped
sea salt

FOR THE HERBY YOGHURT
2 tablespoons olive oil
handful of coriander (about
   5–10g), roughly chopped,
   plus extra leaves to serve
5 tablespoons coconut
   yoghurt
juice of 1 lemon

QUICK PAN-FRIED TOFU AND HERBY YOGHURT SANDWICH

1. Start by making a quick pickle from the cucumber. Mix the apple cider vinegar, maple syrup and a large pinch of sea salt in a medium bowl, add the cucumber ribbons and toss them in the mixture so that they're coated. Leave to sit for 10 minutes, stirring occasionally, while you prepare the rest of the sandwich.

2. Put the oil into a large frying pan over a high heat. Once hot, add your tofu and fry for 3 minutes, until golden, then flip and do the same on the other side.

3. To make the herby yoghurt, mix the olive oil, chopped coriander, yoghurt, lemon juice and the pickling liquid from the cucumber, until smooth and creamy. Season to taste.

4. Either serve as a sandwich, or on toast. For the sandwich, spread the yoghurt mix on to two slices of the sourdough and top each slice with the tofu and pickled cucumber. Sprinkle the chilli over the top along with the extra coriander leaves, then top with the other slices of sourdough. Serve with extra sauce on the side. For the toast, simply toast the sourdough and pile everything up on individual slices.

Serves 2
Time 10 minutes

What's not to love – guacamole but with added protein, to make it more filling and more of a whole meal. This has only six ingredients, it takes five minutes and it's always super satisfying.

1 ripe avocado, peeled and
  stoned
1 × 400g tin of chickpeas,
  drained and rinsed
2 tablespoons olive oil, plus
  extra to drizzle
handful of coriander, (about
  5–10g), finely chopped, plus
  extra to serve
1 small red onion, finely
  chopped
juice of 2 limes
2–4 slices of sourdough
  (depending on whether you
  want an open sandwich or
  not)
sea salt and black pepper

TO SERVE (OPTIONAL)
lettuce leaves
cucumber slices

SMASHED CHICKPEA GUACAMOLE SANDWICH

1. Smash the avocado in a bowl with the back of a fork until it's nice and smooth. Add the chickpeas and smash again until they're coarsely crushed into the avocado but haven't turned into a paste. Stir in the olive oil, coriander, red onion and lime juice, and season to taste.

2. Either serve as a sandwich, or on toast. For the sandwich, spread the chickpea guacamole on two slices of the sourdough, cover with lettuce leaves and cucumber slices, if using, then top with the other slices of sourdough. For the toast, simply toast the sourdough and drizzle over a little oil, then pile your chickpea guacamole on top.

MAKE IT DINNER
This is a brilliant jacket potato
filling too for a quick midweek
supper.

Serves 2
Time 20 minutes

Anything with potatoes, peanut butter and chilli is a winner for me. This recipe has everything you need – it's equal parts zesty, creamy, crunchy, spicy and just so very satisfying. I've popped it into the lunch chapter, as it's such a speedy, energising meal, but it's perfect for dinner too.

200g baby potatoes, quartered
1 tablespoon olive oil, plus extra to toss the potatoes
½ × block of firm tofu (about 150g), cut into bite-sized chunks (about 2cm)
¼ white or Chinese cabbage (about 150g), cored and leaves shredded
1 carrot, grated
handful of coriander (about 25g), finely chopped, plus extra to serve
2 red chillies, finely chopped, plus extra to serve
sea salt and black pepper

FOR THE SAUCE
4 tablespoons smooth peanut butter
2 teaspoons maple syrup
100g coconut yoghurt
grated zest and juice of 2 limes

CRUNCHY SATAY POTATO SALAD

1. Put the potatoes into a saucepan of boiling water with a pinch of salt and simmer for 15 minutes, covered. Drain and let steam dry for 5 minutes, then toss with a little olive oil and salt.

2. Meanwhile, put the oil into a frying pan over a high heat, add the tofu and fry for 10 minutes, until golden and crisp, turning so that each side is coloured. Remove from the pan and leave to cool completely.

3. To make the sauce, whisk all the ingredients together along with 2 tablespoons of water and season to taste.

4. To serve, place the tofu, potatoes, cabbage, carrots and coriander into sections in a bowl, top with a little extra chilli, then pour the sauce over the salad to serve.

'If you really don't like
beetroot, you can swap it for
grilled broccoli or cauliflower.
They're just as delicious,
though not quite as colourful.'

Serves 2
Time 15 minutes

I know beetroots aren't everyone's favourite veg, but trust me on this one, you have to try this salad. I say salad but really it's more than that. It's the scooping of harissa yoghurt with lots of herbs, sweet beets and zesty lentils with toasted pitta that does it for me – it's just so creamy, juicy and satisfying. A perfect lunch!

1 tablespoon olive oil

½ teaspoon cumin seeds

2 garlic cloves, finely sliced

2 large, pre-cooked beetroot (about 125g), cut into thin wedges

1 × 400g tin of green lentils, drained and rinsed, or 1 × 250g packet of cooked Puy lentils

½ bunch of coriander (about 10–15g), finely chopped, plus extra to serve

½ bunch of dill (about 10–15g), finely chopped, plus extra to serve (optional)

grated zest and juice of 1 lemon

100g coconut yoghurt

1 tablespoon harissa

sea salt and black pepper

pitta bread, toasted, to serve

CREAMY BEETROOT, LENTIL AND YOGHURT SALAD WITH TOASTED PITTA

1. Put the oil into a frying pan over a medium heat. Once warm, add the cumin seeds, garlic and cooked beetroot and fry for 3–4 minutes until the beetroot is tender and crisp around the outside and the oil smells fragrant, then pour the contents into a bowl.

2. Put the frying pan back over a medium heat and add the lentils, herbs, lemon zest (keeping a little back for serving) and juice and season to taste, cooking until warmed through.

3. To serve spoon the coconut yoghurt over serving plates and swirl through the harissa. Top with the lentil mixture, then the cooked beetroot and drizzle over the garlicky cumin oil before finishing with the reserved herbs and reserved lemon zest. Serve with the toasted pitta on the side and use it to mop up the harissa yoghurt.

Serves 2
Time 15 minutes

This is the epitome of healthy made simple – it's very quick, looks beautiful, tastes delicious and is packed with goodness. The contrast of textures really makes this salad; you've got salad leaves, chives and avocado tossed in a simple mustard and lemon dressing on the bottom, then a crunchy mix of chickpeas, seeds and sourdough on the top.

1 large, soft lettuce (butter lettuce is brilliant) or salad leaves (about 150g)
½ bunch of chives (about 10–15g), finely chopped
1 ripe avocado, finely sliced
flaky sea salt

FOR THE DRESSING
grated zest and juice of 1 lemon
½ bunch of chives (about 10–15g), finely chopped
4 tablespoons olive oil
½ teaspoon Dijon mustard

FOR THE CRUNCHY TOPPING
1 × 400g tin of chickpeas, drained and rinsed
handful of sunflower seeds (about 25g)
handful of pumpkin seeds (about 25g)
2 slices of sourdough (about 75g), crusts on, torn into bite-sized pieces
1 tablespoon olive oil

AVOCADO AND BUTTER LETTUCE SALAD WITH A CRUNCHY PROTEIN TOPPING

1. First make the crunchy topping. Preheat the oven to 200°C fan.

2. Put the chickpeas, sunflower seeds, pumpkin seeds and sourdough on to a large baking tray. Drizzle with the oil, scatter over a big pinch of sea salt and bake in the oven for 10–15 minutes until golden, tossing halfway through. Leave to cool completely.

3. Meanwhile, make the dressing by whisking the ingredients together in a small bowl. Season to taste.

4. Toss the lettuce, chives and avocado together and place in a serving bowl, then toss through half of the dressing. Sprinkle the crunchy topping on top and finish with a drizzle of the dressing.

'This is a brilliant side salad when you're cooking for a big group of people, especially in the summer. Serve it alongside lots of delicious dips, grains, veggie burgers.'

Serves 2
Time 20 minutes

These feel-good bowls are genuinely rays of sunshine! I'm normally not a big fan of fruit in savoury food, but I'll always make an exception for this pineapple and mango salsa with chilli, mint and pomegranate. It's bursting with colour and flavour and instantly brings this simple recipe together.

100g quinoa

3 tablespoons olive oil, plus extra for the salsa

½ × block of tofu (about 150g), cut into small cubes (optional)

1 mango (about 250g), peeled and finely diced

½ pineapple (about 500g), peeled and finely diced

1 red chilli, finely chopped

bunch of mint (about 25g), leaves picked and finely chopped

large handful of pomegranate seeds (about 50g)

½ small cucumber, finely diced

sea salt and black pepper

MANGO, MINT AND CHILLI SUNSHINE BOWLS

1. Cook the quinoa in salted water according to the instructions on the pack, then drain and leave to cool on a separate plate while you prep the rest of the recipe.

2. Put 1 tablespoon of the oil into a frying pan over a high heat, add the tofu and fry for 5–8 minutes, until golden brown all over. Remove from the pan and leave to cool.

3. To make the salsa, simply put the mango, pineapple, chilli, mint and pomegranate seeds into a bowl and toss with a sprinkling of salt and the remaining 2 tablespoons of olive oil.

4. To serve, place the quinoa in a serving bowl, followed by the cucumber, tofu, and salsa. Season to taste.

'I've included tofu in these for a little protein, but lentils make for a great swap. Simply stir a tin of drained, rinsed green lentils into the cooked quinoa before serving. If you do that and use pre-made quinoa, then it becomes a no-cook recipe too!'

Serves 2
Time 15 minutes

Fresh spring rolls have always been one of my favourite foods. They're deliciously light, packed with flavour and I love how healthy and vibrant they always feel. I've used almond butter in the dipping sauce but any smooth nut butter or tahini (to make it nut free) would work brilliantly.

50g rice vermicelli noodles

1 teaspoon olive oil

½ bunch of coriander (about 10–15g), finely chopped

½ bunch of flat-leaf parsley (about 10–15g), finely chopped

1 small red pepper, finely sliced

1 carrot, grated or cut into thin batons

½ small cucumber, cut into thin batons

juice of 1 lime

1 tablespoon tamari or soy sauce

4 rice paper wrappers

FOR THE DIPPING SAUCE

3 tablespoons almond butter

grated zest and juice of 1 lime

1 tablespoon tamari or soy sauce

HERBY SUMMER ROLLS

1. Cook the noodles according to the instructions on the pack. Drain well and rinse under cold running water, then toss with the olive oil. Meanwhile make the dipping sauce by whisking the ingredients together in a small bowl.

2. Next, toss the coriander, parsley, pepper, carrot, cucumber, lime and tamari in another bowl and season to taste.

3. Prepare the rolls. Fill a wide shallow bowl with cold water, wide enough to submerge the rice paper wrappers. Dip a rice paper wrapper into the water until it's pliable (or according to the pack instructions). Lay it out flat on a clean work surface and put a quarter of the rice noodles into the centre of the wrap, then top the noodles with some of the mixed vegetables leaving a small border around the outside.

4. Fold the sides of the wrapper in, like you would do with a burrito, wrapping the two sides across the filling first, followed by the ends. Continue with the remaining mix and serve with the dipping sauce.

'To make it nut free, simply swap the cashews for sunflower seeds; it's just as delicious.'

Serves 2
Time 15 minutes

This is the kind of meal I cook both for myself and my kids on repeat. The whole family love it, it's especially quick to make and it's still loaded with veg. Using edamame, peas and cashews really ups the plant protein too, so you've got almost 20g per serving. I've popped it in the lunch chapter, as it's a great hot, filling option when you're at home, but it works brilliantly as a midweek supper too.

2 servings of pasta (about
    75g per person), I use
    wholewheat
100g frozen peas
100g frozen edamame
large handful of baby spinach
    (about 50g), roughly
    chopped
sea salt and black pepper

FOR THE HERBY GREEN
SAUCE
50g cashews
75ml oat milk
1 tablespoon olive oil
½ teaspoon Dijon or
    wholegrain mustard
grated zest and juice of
    1 lemon
½ bunch of coriander (about
    10–15g), finely chopped,
    plus extra to serve
½ bunch of dill, basil or parsley
    (about 10–15g), finely
    chopped, plus extra to
    serve
small handful (about 25g) of
    baby spinach
sea salt and black pepper

MY GO-TO GREEN PASTA

1. Cook the pasta in boiling water with a pinch of salt, according to the instructions on the pack. Add the frozen peas, edamame and spinach for the last minute or two, so that the veg is tender and the spinach has wilted. Drain and leave to cool for a minute or two, then put everything back into the pan.

2. While the pasta cooks, make the sauce. Simply put all the ingredients into a high-speed blender with a generous sprinkling of salt and pepper and blitz until you have a smooth sauce. Add an extra splash of milk or olive oil if needed to get it to a consistency you like and check the seasoning.

3. Pour the sauce over the pan of pasta and mix until it's coated. This can be served warm or cold, depending on the time of year and your preference. Season to taste and serve with an extra drizzle of olive oil and the extra herbs.

Serves 2
Time 15 minutes

I've always loved a rainbow-style bowl, I think it's the mix of rice, pickled onions, chilli and spring onions that does it for me. The miso mushrooms give this one a deliciously deep, intense flavour. If you're not a mushroom person, simply switch them for finely diced aubergines.

1 red onion, finely sliced
juice of 2 limes, plus extra
    wedges to serve
2 servings of white jasmine
    rice (about 50g per person)
200g mushrooms (I like using
    chestnut and button), finely
    sliced
1 tablespoon olive oil
½ teaspoon brown rice miso
    paste
100g frozen edamame
6 spring onions, finely
    chopped
2 tablespoons sesame seeds
1 red chilli, finely sliced
sea salt

FOR THE DRESSING
2 tablespoons olive oil
1 teaspoon brown rice miso
    paste
1 red chilli, deseeded and
    finely chopped

MISO MUSHROOM BOWLS

1. Start by making the pickled onions. Put the red onion and lime juice into a bowl along with a pinch of salt and set aside for at least 10 minutes or until needed.

2. Cook the jasmine rice according to the instructions on the pack, adding the edamame for the last minute or two, so that they cook through but keep their bite, then drain and set aside until the rice is cool to the touch.

3. Make your miso mushrooms. Put the mushrooms into a bowl, then add the oil and miso and massage the mushrooms so they're coated in the mix. Put a large frying pan over a medium–high heat and add the mushrooms. Fry for 4–5 minutes until golden and soft. Remove from the heat and leave to cool.

4. Make the dressing by whisking all the ingredients together in a bowl along with the pickling liquid from the onions. Season to taste and set aside.

5. Mix the rice and edamame with half of the dressing and divide it between two serving bowls. In sections, top the rice with the mushrooms, spring onions and pickled onions, then sprinkle over the red chilli and sesame seeds, pour over the remaining dressing and serve the lime wedges on the side.

Serves 2
Time 15 minutes

If you want a simple, satisfying, healthy lunch that works brilliantly on the go, then this is what you need. It's a quick, fuss-free option that works so well in a lunchbox. You can easily double the quantities and use it as the base of your lunches all week.

2 servings of pasta; I like
    farfalle (about 75g per
    person)
½ × block of firm tofu (about
    150g), cut into tiny pea-
    sized pieces
1 small cucumber, halved
    lengthways, cored and cut
    into cubes
1 small jar of sun-dried
    tomatoes in oil, drained and
    finely chopped
100g cherry tomatoes, halved
1 small red onion, finely
    chopped
bunch of basil (about 25g),
    finely chopped, plus extra
    leaves to serve
large handful of pitted black
    olives (about 50g)
sea salt and black pepper

FOR THE DRESSING
grated zest and juice of
    1 lemon
3 tablespoons oil from the
    sun-dried tomato jar
2 teaspoons maple syrup

SUN-DRIED TOMATO, BASIL AND OLIVE PASTA SALAD

1. Cook the pasta in salted water in a large saucepan according to the instructions on the pack. Place the tofu in a steaming basket on top of the pan and steam it as the pasta cooks.

2. Once al dente, drain the pasta and rinse with cold water, until the pasta is cool to touch. Leave the tofu to one side to cool.

3. Mix the dressing ingredients together in a small bowl and season with salt and pepper to taste.

4. Toss the cool pasta and tofu with the cucumber, sun-dried tomatoes, cherry tomatoes, red onion, most of the chopped basil, the olives, and the dressing. Serve with some basil leaves on top.

Serves 2
Time 15 minutes

This is my favourite lunch when I'm working from home. You need one saucepan, about 10 minutes (15 at a stretch), and you've got a plate that's packed with brilliant colours, textures and flavours. It's the perfect meal for long-lasting energy too, with a great mix of plant protein, healthy fats and carbs.

2 servings of soba noodles
(about 60g per person)
1 × block of medium-firm tofu
(about 300g), cut into small
cubes (about 1cm)
½ bunch of flat-leaf parsley
(about 10–15g), finely
chopped
½ bunch of chives (about
10–15g), finely chopped
6 spring onions, finely
chopped
grated zest and juice of
2 limes, plus extra to serve
pinch of dried chilli flakes
1 garlic clove, grated or
crushed
2 tablespoons tamari or soy
sauce
1 tablespoon olive oil, plus
extra to serve
1 ripe avocado, cut into chunks
sea salt

15-MINUTE HERBY AVOCADO NOODLES

1. Bring a large pan of salted water to the boil and fit a steaming basket on the top of the pan. Cook the noodles in the boiling water according the instructions on the pack and place the tofu in the basket. Place the lid on the pan and cook the two together until the noodles are ready.

2. While they cook, place the herbs, spring onions, lime zest and juice, chilli, garlic, tamari and olive oil in a mixing bowl with a pinch of salt and toss well. Once the noodles are cooked, mix them through the sauce too.

3. Transfer to serving bowls, then scatter the tofu and avocado on the top and finish with a drizzle of olive oil. Serve with lime wedges on the side.

Serves 2
Time 15 minutes

This is a shortcut recipe for a quick, creamy, deeply flavoursome dhal. Traditional black dhal uses black urad dhal (lentils), but cooking those from scratch takes a long time, so we've swapped them for pre-cooked Puy lentils so that you can get lunch on the table in 15-minutes, making it an easy option for a quick lunch. The chilli, ginger, red onion and coriander give it a punchy flavour that's equally warming and invigorating.

1 tablespoon olive oil

1 medium red onion, finely chopped

small chunk of ginger (about 20g/2cm), peeled and finely chopped

1 long green chilli, finely chopped

1 × 250g pack of cooked Puy lentils or 1 × 400g tin of green lentils, drained and rinsed

1 heaped tablespoon tomato purée

125ml coconut cream, plus extra to serve

2 teaspoons medium curry powder

2 large handfuls of spinach (about 100g)

juice of ½ lemon

½ bunch of coriander (about 10–15g), roughly chopped

sea salt

15-MINUTE BLACK DHAL

1. Warm the olive oil in a saucepan set over a medium heat. Set aside about a third of each of the chopped onion, ginger and chilli, then add the remainder to the pan. Cook for 8–10 minutes, until soft and fragrant.

2. While the onion is cooking, add 2 tablespoons of lentils, the tomato purée, coconut cream, curry powder and a pinch of salt to a food processor or mini chopper and blitz until completely smooth.

3. Add the spice paste to the onions and cook for another minute, then add the remaining lentils and 200ml of boiling water. Bring to a simmer then add the spinach and lemon juice, stirring until the spinach has wilted. Taste to check the seasoning and adjust as needed.

4. Divide the dhal between serving bowls and scatter over the reserved onion, ginger and chilli, followed by the coriander, a pinch of salt and an extra spoonful of coconut cream.

'If you don't have any coconut cream, swap it for coconut yoghurt, stirring it all in at the end.'

I find that making delicious speedy salads for lunch is relatively easy, but knowing how to make a warm, nourishing bowl at lunchtime can be a little harder, as those stew-type recipes tend to have longer cook times. This is my super-quick lunchtime stew – all the cosiness and flavour you want in just 15 minutes!

1 tablespoon olive oil

2 shallots, thinly sliced

1 × 400ml tin of coconut milk

1 × 400g tin of chickpeas, drained and rinsed

small chunk of ginger (about 10g/1cm), peeled and cut into matchsticks

1 bird's-eye chilli, thinly sliced

1 tablespoon white miso paste

1 teaspoon ground turmeric

1 teaspoon tamari

1 vegetable stock cube

100g frozen edamame beans

2 limes, juice of 1, the other cut into wedges to serve

sea salt and black pepper

15-MINUTE CHICKPEA, EDAMAME AND MISO STEW

1. Warm the oil in a sauté pan or large saucepan set over a medium–high heat. Add the shallot and cook for 5 minutes, stirring frequently until golden all over.

2. Add the coconut milk, chickpeas, ginger, chilli, miso, turmeric, tamari and stock cube. Bring to the boil then reduce the heat, cover with a lid and simmer for 10 minutes.

3. About a minute before the stew is ready, add the edamame beans, bring back to a simmer and cook for another minute or so, until the beans are tender.

4. Stir in the lime juice and season to taste, then divide between serving bowls and serve with lime wedges.

'I love this just as it is but it's also delicious with rice or noodles to make it a little more filling.'

Serves 2
Time 20 minutes

I had to include this in here, especially for anyone new to our cookbooks. This is my go-to dressing – I can't even begin to count the number of times I've made it, my sister and I actually call it 'the dressing'. It's a simple salad but I could genuinely eat it every day.

4 large handfuls of mixed greens (about 200g), I love kale, rocket and spinach
1½ tablespoons olive oil, plus extra for toasting the seeds
juice of ½ lemon
1 ripe avocado, diced
2 slices of sourdough
1 small garlic clove, peeled
handful of sunflower seeds (about 30g)
sea salt and black pepper

FOR THE CREAMY CASHEW DRESSING
40g sunflower seeds
60g cashews
100ml oat milk
1 tablespoon Dijon mustard
1 tablespoon nutritional yeast (optional)
3 tablespoons olive oil
juice of ½ lemon

MY EVERY SINGLE DAY SALAD

1. Remove any thick stems from the kale, if using, and place the remaining leaves in a large bowl along with the rest of the greens. If you're using rocket, hold this back until the end. Add the olive oil, lemon juice and a pinch of salt and massage into the leaves using your hands, until they soften.

2. To make the dressing, put all the ingredients into a high-speed blender. Season well with salt and pepper and blend until smooth and creamy. You might need to let it down with a couple of tablespoons of water.

3. Next, toast the sourdough and rub the raw garlic clove into both sides. Cut each slice into bite-sized chunks.

4. Put a large frying pan over a medium heat, add the sunflower seeds, and toast for 3–4 minutes, until just golden. Add about a teaspoon or so of olive oil, followed by the sourdough, and cook for about 2 minutes, until crisp and golden. Season with salt and pepper.

5. To serve, add the rocket, croutons, seeds and avocado to the greens, pour over the dressing and toss everything together.

CHAPTER 3

MIDWEEK SUPPERS

This chapter is about getting delicious flavours packed with goodness on the table in less time, with less work and with fewer ingredients. It's simple cooking at its best. In thinking about these recipes, I wanted to help you create a moment of calm in a busy week – a chance for a little self-care, and a way to do something nourishing for yourself. It's easy to make a piece of toast or order a takeaway, but these recipes really aren't that much harder and don't take much longer, yet they give you so much more.

I make this a lot when I've got a girlfriend coming over for supper. It's speedy, simple and full of beautiful flavours, yet so easy to bring together. I tend to serve it with a peppery rocket and avocado salad on the side. Swap the cavolo nero for any seasonal green, or the walnuts for pine nuts.

2 servings of spaghetti (about 75g per person)

large handful of walnuts (about 75g)

2 tablespoons olive oil, plus extra to serve

2 garlic cloves, thinly sliced

½ teaspoon dried chilli flakes

3–4 large handfuls of cavolo nero (about 150–200g), leaves stripped from the stalks and roughly sliced

juice of ½ lemon

large handful of rocket (about 50g)

sea salt and black pepper

CAVOLO NERO AND WALNUT SPAGHETTI

1. Bring a large saucepan of salted water to the boil, add the spaghetti and cook according to the instructions on the pack or until al dente.

2. While the pasta is cooking, set a large frying pan over a medium heat and add the walnuts. Cook for 4–5 minutes, stirring often, until golden. Tip the toasted walnuts into a high-speed blender and set aside.

3. Pour the olive oil into the frying pan, add the garlic and chilli and cook for 30 seconds, then add the cavolo nero and cook for 4–5 minutes, stirring occasionally, until wilted. Add everything to the high-speed blender.

4. Drain the pasta, reserving a mugful of cooking water, and add about 150ml to the blender, along with a big pinch of salt and lots of pepper. Blitz until smooth then spoon into the pan and add the cooked pasta. Warm gently over a low heat, adding the remaining pasta water – there should be about 125ml left – and stir until you have a creamy green sauce. Add the lemon juice and season to taste.

5. Divide the pasta between serving plates, scatter over the rocket, drizzle with a little more olive oil and add plenty of black pepper.

Serves 2
Time 30 minutes

With just five ingredients – courgettes, garlic, chilli, lemon and linguine, this is one of those meals where you can't believe how good simple cooking can taste. If you don't have linguine, lots of other pasta shapes work, such as trofie, casarecce, orecchiette, penne or fusilli – I particularly love orecchiette.

4 tablespoons olive oil, plus
  extra to serve
4 garlic cloves, thinly sliced
½–1 teaspoon dried chilli
  flakes, plus extra to serve
4 courgettes (about 750g), half
  cut into 5mm rounds, half
  cut into 5mm half moons
2 servings of linguine (about
  75g per person)
grated zest of 1 lemon
sea salt and black pepper

SLOW-COOKED COURGETTE, OLIVE OIL AND CHILLI LINGUINE

1. Warm the olive oil in a large frying pan set over a medium–low heat. Add the garlic and chilli and cook for 1–2 minutes, until just golden. Next add the courgettes along with a big pinch of salt and cook for 25 minutes, until jammy and translucent, stirring occasionally to make sure nothing catches.

2. Meanwhile, bring a large saucepan of salted water to the boil, add the linguine and cook until al dente. Drain, reserving a mugful of the cooking water.

3. Tip the pasta into the frying pan, adding a splash of the cooking water – about 4 tablespoons, and stir everything together until you have a silky-smooth sauce. Season to taste with salt and pepper.

4. To serve, divide the pasta between serving plates, scatter over the lemon zest, drizzle with olive oil and sprinkle with extra chilli flakes, salt and pepper.

'Finishing the dish with good quality olive oil makes the world of difference in flavour.'

'To ensure this cooks quickly, make sure you don't cut the sweet potato wedges too thick or they won't be perfectly tender.'

Serves 2
Time 30 minutes

Sweet potato dishes have been a staple of mine for a decade. For this one, I've given a favourite a little refresh, adding the quick pickled red onions for a great tang (and a fab pink colour!), crispy lentils to ensure a great bite and the ginger, coriander and yoghurt dressing to make it lovely and creamy. You can always sprinkle over a little chilli if you want some more heat too.

2 sweet potatoes, cut lengthways into thin wedges (about 1.5cm thick)
1 × 400g tin of green lentils, drained and rinsed
1 teaspoon cumin seeds
1 teaspoon garam masala
4 tablespoons olive oil
2 large handfuls of kale (about 100g), leaves stripped from the stalks and torn into bite-sized pieces
1 red onion, thinly sliced
juice of 1 lime
sea salt and black pepper

FOR THE CORIANDER AND GINGER YOGHURT DRESSING
2 bunches of coriander (stalks and leaves, about 50g)
4 tablespoons coconut yoghurt
small chunk of ginger (about 30g/3cm), peeled and roughly chopped
juice of 1 lime

SWEET POTATO AND CRISPY LENTIL BOWLS WITH CORIANDER AND GINGER YOGHURT

1. Preheat the oven to 200°C fan. In a large mixing bowl toss the sweet potato, lentils, cumin seeds, garam masala, 3 tablespoons of the olive oil and season generously. Tip into a large baking tray and roast in the oven for 25 minutes, stirring once, until the sweet potatoes are tender and the lentils are crispy.

2. Meanwhile, quickly pickle the onions. Put the onion, half the lime juice and 1 teaspoon of salt into a small bowl, mix well and set aside to pickle.

3. Next, prep the salad. Add the kale to the now empty mixing bowl, along with the remaining olive oil and a pinch of salt. Massage with your fingers for a minute or so, until the kale has softened. Leave to one side.

4. To make the dressing, set aside a few of the coriander leaves then put the remaining stalks and leaves into a high-speed blender with the coconut yoghurt, ginger, lime juice and a pinch of salt and blitz until smooth. Check the seasoning and adjust as needed.

5. To serve, divide the cooked sweet potato between two bowls, then add the kale, crispy lentils, pickled onions, drizzle over the dressing, and scatter over the reserved coriander leaves.

Serves 2

Time 30 minutes

I imagine lots of people might skip past this recipe – roasted shallots don't tend to carry the same appeal as veggies like sweet potatoes, but roasting them in their skins ensures they're perfectly sweet and tender, so please trust me on this one, it's a must and one of my favourite recipes in the book. It feels like one giant, very cosy, nourishing hug.

5 shallots, quartered lengthways, keeping the root intact and the skin on

3 tablespoons olive oil, plus extra to serve (see tip below)

4 garlic cloves, skin on

1 teaspoon thyme leaves, finely chopped, or 1 teaspoon dried thyme

pinch of dried chilli flakes (optional)

2 leeks, sliced

120g green beans, trimmed

1 × 400g tin of butter beans

2 large handfuls of baby spinach (about 100g), roughly chopped

1 tablespoon white wine vinegar

grated zest of 1 lemon

sea salt and black pepper

sourdough toast, to serve (optional)

'You can swap the spinach for kale, cavolo nero or Swiss chard, and make sure to use a really good quality olive oil for the drizzle at the end, it makes all the difference.'

COSY ROASTED SHALLOT AND BUTTER BEAN BOWLS

1. Preheat the oven to 180°C fan. Toss the shallots with a tablespoon of the olive oil and a pinch of salt. Place on a baking tray, cut-side down, add the garlic cloves and roast in the oven for 25–30 minutes, until soft and caramelised.

2. Warm the remaining 2 tablespoons of oil in a large frying pan or shallow casserole, over a medium–low heat. Add the thyme, chilli flakes (if using), leeks and a pinch of salt and cook for 10 minutes, until the leeks have softened but not coloured.

3. Next, add the green beans and the butter beans, along with the liquid from the tin. Bring to a gentle boil and cook for 4–5 minutes, until most of the liquid has reduced. Stir in the spinach, and allow to wilt, then add the white wine vinegar and season to taste.

4. When the shallots are ready and cool enough to handle, peel their skins off and stir the flesh into the beans. Peel the garlic, gently mash it with a fork (it should be very tender) and stir it into the beans too.

5. To serve, divide the braised beans between serving bowls, top with a generous drizzle of olive oil, the lemon zest and plenty of pepper. This is delicious as it is or served with some sourdough toast.

'This keeps really well so
you can always double the
quantities and use the second
half for lunch the next day.'

Serves 2
Time 25 minutes

With around 25g of plant protein in each portion, these zesty green bowls are perfect for keeping you energised. The good news is that they taste amazing too – the pan-fried chilli and garlic coupled with the lemon zest add fantastic flavour. It's the kind of recipe I make on a Monday night, when I need to feel my best ahead of a busy week.

100g quinoa
200ml hot vegetable stock
120g frozen peas or petit pois
120g frozen edamame
50g mixed seeds (I use
    sesame, pumpkin and
    sunflower)
1 head of broccoli, chopped
    into bite-sized florets
5 tablespoons olive oil
2 garlic cloves, thinly sliced
1–2 bird's eye chillies, thinly
    sliced
grated zest and juice of
    1 lemon
sea salt and black pepper

———

NOTE
If you need to be super-speedy, you can cook the broccoli all at once, it may just lose a little of its texture.

GARLICKY BROCCOLI AND CHILLI PROTEIN BOWLS

1. Pour the quinoa and stock into a medium saucepan, bring to the boil, then cover with a lid and reduce the heat to low. Simmer for 10 minutes, adding the peas and edamame beans for the final 2 minutes. The liquid should all have been absorbed at this point, if not drain off any excess. Remove from the heat and leave to stand.

2. While the quinoa cooks, place a large frying pan over a medium–low heat, add the seeds and cook for 5 minutes, until golden. Remove from the pan and set aside.

3. Increase the heat to high and add half the broccoli to the dry frying pan —make sure the pan isn't overcrowded otherwise the broccoli won't char properly. Cook for 5–6 minutes, shaking the pan every now and again, until the broccoli is charred all over, then remove and set aside. Repeat with the remaining broccoli (see Note opposite).

4. Turn the heat down to low and add 1 tablespoon of the olive oil to the pan, quickly followed by the garlic and chilli. Cook for 2–3 minutes, until crisp. Remove the pan from the heat and stir the broccoli into the garlic and chilli.

5. To make the dressing, whisk together the remaining 4 tablespoons of olive oil, the lemon juice, a big pinch of salt and some pepper. Fluff the quinoa with a fork and stir through the dressing. Check the seasoning and adjust as needed. To serve, divide the quinoa between bowls, then scatter over the seeds, charred broccoli and lemon zest.

Serves 2
Time 20 minutes

I've always loved this style of nourishing rainbow bowl, which is packed with all sorts of different colours and textures. As with the zesty green protein bowls, this recipe has over 25g of plant protein in it, making it a brilliant meal on days where you need lots of energy. The tahini, maple syrup and lime dressing gives the dish a lovely creaminess, while the slices of cucumber and radish add a gentle crunch.

1 × block of firm tofu (about 300g)
1 tablespoon olive oil
100g quinoa
200ml hot vegetable stock
100g radishes, finely sliced
1 small cucumber, deseeded and finely diced
1 ripe avocado, diced
sea salt and black pepper

FOR THE DRESSING
6 tablespoons olive oil
2 limes, juice of 1, the other cut in half
2 tablespoons maple syrup
4 tablespoons tahini (see Note below)

CRUNCHY TOFU, QUINOA AND TAHINI PROTEIN BOWLS

1. Pat the tofu dry with kitchen paper and cut it into bite-sized pieces. Warm the olive oil in a large frying pan set over a medium–high heat. Add the tofu and cook for 10–12 minutes, turning every 2 minutes or so, until golden and crisp all over.

2. While the tofu cooks, pour the quinoa and vegetable stock into a small saucepan. Bring to the boil, then cover with a lid and simmer for 10 minutes. Remove from the heat and leave to stand until everything else is ready, draining any excess liquid first.

3. To make the dressing, whisk together all the ingredients in a bowl with a big pinch of salt, some pepper and about a tablespoon of water. It should be the consistency of single cream so add more water as necessary.

4. Fluff the quinoa with a fork and stir through a third of the dressing. Season with salt and pepper then spoon into serving bowls. Toss another third of the dressing with the tofu, then pour the tofu and dressing over the quinoa. Add the radish, cucumber and avocado and drizzle over the last of the dressing.

5. Season and serve with the lime halves to squeeze over the top.

NOTE
Keep any leftover dressing in a jar in the fridge for up to two weeks.

Serves 2
Time 30 minutes

My husband and I like going out for Indian food and whenever we get a date night it's what we head for. I've always loved the palak paneer sauce and wanted to try to make a simple, at-home recipe inspired by the dish, but swapping the paneer for tofu to make it fully plant-based. I'd definitely put this recipe in the 'you need to make this' bucket; it's super creamy and warming with a lovely hit of ginger, garlic and chilli in every mouthful.

5 large handfuls of baby
    spinach (about 250g)
2 tablespoons olive oil
1 teaspoon cumin seeds
1 onion, diced
4 garlic cloves, grated or finely
    chopped
small chunk of ginger (about
    40g/5cm), peeled and
    grated
½ teaspoon hot chilli powder
½ teaspoon garam masala
2 handfuls of cherry tomatoes
    (about 125g), roughly
    chopped
sea salt

FOR THE TOFU
3 tablespoons nutritional yeast
3 tablespoons olive oil
1 × block of firm tofu (about
    300g), drained, dried and
    cut into 2cm cubes

CREAMY PANEER-INSPIRED TOFU

1. Warm a shallow casserole dish or large frying pan on a medium–high heat. Add three quarters of the spinach with a splash of water, cover with a lid and leave it to wilt, about 2–3 minutes, stirring a couple of times. Once wilted, tip the spinach into a high-speed blender with 150ml of water and blitz until smooth. Set aside.

2. Set the pan back over a medium heat and add the olive oil. Once warm, add the cumin seeds and cook for 30 seconds, until fragrant. Next, add the onion, garlic and ginger and a pinch of salt and cook on a medium heat for 10 minutes, until golden and translucent.

3. Meanwhile, prepare the tofu. In a bowl mix the nutritional yeast and oil until they form a paste, then stir through the tofu. Set a large frying pan over a medium–low heat and once warm add the tofu. Cook for 8–10 minutes, turning every 2 minutes, so that it's crisp and golden all over, then remove from the heat and set aside.

4. Add the chilli powder, garam masala and tomatoes to the onion mixture and cook on a medium heat for 5 minutes, until the tomatoes have started to break down. Roughly chop the remaining spinach, then stir it in, along with the blended spinach mix.

5. Once everything has come together and the spinach has wilted, season to taste and stir through the crispy tofu. Serve as it is, with rice or wholemeal flatbreads.

Serves 2
Time 30 minutes

My sister and I swapped recipe ideas throughout the Covid lockdowns, and it was her that inspired me to start roasting cabbage. I'd never made it before but instantly loved it. It's not a vegetable that we tend to gravitate to, but it's absolutely delicious. This is also very simple to make, it's a one-tray wonder that comes together with only a tiny amount of prep.

1 small hispi cabbage, cut into quarters lengthways, keeping the root intact, then each quarter cut into 6 wedges

1 aubergine, cut into half moons (about 2cm thick)

1 × 400g tin of chickpeas, drained and rinsed

4 garlic cloves, skin on

3 tablespoons olive oil

2 tablespoons coconut yoghurt

1 tablespoon maple syrup

2 tablespoons tahini

grated zest and juice of ½ lemon

1 tablespoon sumac, to serve (optional, don't worry if you don't have it)

sea salt and pepper

CRISPY ONE-TRAY HISPI CABBAGE WITH GARLIC YOGHURT

1. Preheat the oven to 180°C fan.

2. Put the cabbage, aubergine, chickpeas and garlic cloves onto a large baking tray, then pour over the olive oil and season generously. Roast for 25 minutes, stirring halfway through the cooking time, until the vegetables are tender and the chickpeas slightly crisp.

3. To make the dressing, whisk together the coconut yoghurt, maple syrup, tahini and lemon juice and season generously with salt and pepper.

4. Once the vegetables are cooked, squeeze the inside of the garlic cloves into the dressing (they should be perfectly tender) and use a fork to roughly crush and mix into the dressing. Taste to check the seasoning and adjust as needed.

5. Spoon some of the garlic yoghurt over the vegetables (or serve on the side), then scatter over the lemon zest, sumac, if using, and a pinch of salt.

NOTE
The leftover garlic yoghurt will keep in the fridge for up to five days – it's a delicious addition to any salad.

Serves 2
Time 30 minutes

I have a feeling that this will be one of the most popular recipes in the book. It's beautifully fresh and vibrant, with the pomegranates, parsley, lemon and rocket, while the harissa gives it a lovely warmth, and the aubergine and walnuts a little earthiness. I make this for friends a lot and it's always a hit. It's a nice recipe to double up so that you can use the leftovers as an on-the-go lunch.

2 servings of brown basmati rice (about 50g per person)
2 aubergines, cut into thin half moons (about 1cm thick)
1 tablespoon harissa
1 tablespoon olive oil
large handful of walnuts (about 75g), roughly chopped
200g pomegranate seeds
½ bunch of flat-leaf parsley (about 10–15g), roughly chopped
½ bunch of mint (about 10–15g), roughly chopped
large handful of rocket (about 50g)
sea salt and black pepper

FOR THE HARISSA DRESSING
1 teaspoon harissa
2 tablespoons olive oil
juice of ½ lemon

'You can simplify this recipe by using a pouch of pre-cooked rice. That way it's just a really easy tray bake that you toss together. Equally, you can mix and match the grain to add variety: bulgur wheat, giant couscous and pearl barley all work really well.'

HERBY JEWELLED RICE WITH ROASTED AUBERGINE, WALNUTS, MINT AND POMEGRANATE

1. Preheat the oven to 180°C fan.

2. Bring 300ml salted water to the boil in a small saucepan, add the rice then cover with a lid and simmer for 20–25 minutes, until all the water has been absorbed. Leave to stand until everything else is ready and fluff with a fork before serving.

3. Once you've got the rice going, put the aubergine, harissa and olive oil on to a large baking tray and season generously with salt and pepper. Give it a really good stir so that the aubergine is coated in harissa and olive oil (using your hands helps with this!). Roast for 25 minutes, stirring once, until the aubergine is tender.

4. When the aubergine has about 5 minutes left, scatter over the walnuts and return the baking tray to the oven.

5. To serve, toss the cooked aubergine and walnuts with the rice, pomegranate seeds, parsley, mint and rocket. Mix the dressing ingredients, pour over the salad, then taste to check the seasoning and divide between plates.

Serves 2
Time 20 minutes

I love a simple vegetable stir-fry, they're one of the best ways to pack loads of different veggies into your day. With garlic, carrots, spinach, leeks and peas you've got five on your plate in this recipe, plus protein from the quinoa and fantastic flavours from the fresh chilli and ginger.

100g quinoa

200ml hot vegetable stock

3 tablespoons olive oil

2 garlic cloves, finely sliced

small chunk of ginger (about 15g/2cm), peeled and coarsely grated

1–2 bird's eye chillies, finely sliced

2 carrots, thinly sliced or julienned with a julienne peeler

2 leeks, sliced

120g frozen peas or petit pois

2 large handfuls of baby spinach (about 100g)

2 tablespoons tamari or soy sauce

1 tablespoon brown rice wine vinegar

'Switch the veggies up depending on what's in season – sweetcorn, kale and courgettes are all great additions. You can also make double quantities of the crispy garlic and chilli mixture and store it in the fridge for up to five days – just make sure that the veg are covered with olive oil. It's an easy way to add flavour to simple salads, soups and scrambled tofu.'

MY EVERYDAY GINGER AND CHILLI STIR-FRY

1. Tip the quinoa and vegetable stock into a small saucepan, bring to the boil, then cover with a lid and simmer for 10 minutes. Remove from the heat and leave to stand until everything else is ready.

2. Warm 2 tablespoons of the olive oil in a large wok or frying pan set over a medium–high heat. Add the garlic, ginger and chilli and cook for 2–4 minutes, until crispy and golden. Watch the pan carefully so that you don't burn the garlic! Quickly remove the garlic and chilli from the pan using a slotted spoon and set aside on kitchen paper.

3. Add the remaining olive oil, carrot, leeks and peas and cook for 5–6 minutes on a medium heat, until just tender. Stir in the spinach and cook for another minute or so, until the spinach has wilted. Remove the pan from the heat and stir in the tamari and vinegar.

4. Fluff the quinoa through with a fork and divide between serving plates. Spoon over the cooked vegetables and scatter over the crispy garlic mixture.

———

NOTE
My little ones love this – I just keep all the fried chillies for me and my husband!

'The key to getting tofu to taste nice is to properly dry it before it's cooked, that way it'll go lovely and crisp on the outside. The quickest way to do this is just to press it with kitchen roll, if you have a few minutes more then wrap it in paper and weigh it down with a couple of books on top to get more liquid out.'

Sweet beets, rich miso, garlic, maple syrup and greens might sound like an unusual combination, but it works so well. Each flavour balances the other creating a beautiful bowl of comforting, nourishing, rainbow goodness! If you find beets a little earthy normally, I'd really recommend giving this a go, as you don't get any of that coming through here.

3 tablespoons olive oil

1 × block of firm tofu (about 300g), drained and cut into bite-sized pieces

2 servings of soba noodles (about 50g per person)

2 garlic cloves, finely sliced or grated

2 large handfuls of kale, spinach or cavolo nero (about 100g), washed and roughly chopped

120g frozen edamame

4 small pre-cooked beetroot (about 250g; see Note), cut into small cubes

3 tablespoons white miso paste

2 tablespoons brown rice vinegar

1 tablespoon maple syrup

3 spring onions, finely sliced

CREAMY BEETROOT, MISO AND TOFU NOODLES

1. Warm 2 tablespoons of the olive oil in a large frying pan set over a medium–high heat. Add the tofu and cook for 10–12 minutes, turning every 2 minutes or so, until crisp and golden all over. Remove from the pan and set aside on kitchen paper.

2. Add the soba noodles to a saucepan of salted boiling water and cook according to the instructions on the pack or until al dente, then drain and rinse with cold water. Leave to one side.

3. Once the tofu is cooked, add the remaining oil to the frying pan, followed by the garlic and cook on a medium heat for 2 minutes, until golden. Add the kale, edamame beans and beetroot and cook for another 3–4 minutes, until tender.

4. While the veg cooks, make the miso sauce. In a bowl, whisk together the miso, brown rice vinegar, maple syrup and about 4 tablespoons of water to loosen – the sauce should be the consistency of single cream.

5. Remove the pan of veg from the heat. Pour in the miso sauce, then add the cooked noodles, tofu and about 3 tablespoons of water. Stir until you have a smooth, creamy sauce. Divide the noodles between plates and top with the spring onions.

NOTE
Make sure you're not buying the beetroot soaked in vinegar as that flavour will be a bit overpowering here.

Serves 2
Time 30 minutes

Whenever I'm feeling a bit run down or coldy, I make these bowls. They're so cosy, comforting, really nourishing and absolutely delicious. You want to serve them with lots of lime so that they're nice and zesty, and be generous with the miso for that rich umami flavour.

4 tablespoons olive oil

1 × block of firm tofu (about 300g), drained and cut into bite-sized pieces

3 shallots, finely sliced

2 garlic cloves, grated or crushed

small chunk of ginger (about 15g/2cm), peeled and grated

200g mixed mushrooms (use shiitake mushrooms if you can find them), sliced

3 tablespoons brown rice miso paste

1 × 400ml tin of coconut milk

500ml hot vegetable stock

2 servings of udon noodles (about 50g per person)

3 large handfuls of baby spinach (about 150g)

grated zest and juice of 1–2 limes

sea salt and black pepper

'This is a great base recipe that you can adjust based on what you've got in the fridge. Add greens, such as bok choy, with the mushrooms, a little turmeric for more colour, or extra chilli for more heat.'

COMFORTING UDON NOODLE BOWLS WITH MUSHROOM AND COCONUT

1. Warm 2 tablespoons of the olive oil in a large frying pan set over a medium–high heat. Add the tofu and cook for 10–12 minutes, turning every 2 minutes or so, until crisp and golden all over. Remove from the pan and set aside on some kitchen paper.

2. While the tofu is cooking, set a large saucepan or wok over a medium–high heat and add the remaining oil. Add the shallots, garlic, ginger and mushrooms and cook for 8–10 minutes, stirring often, until softened and fragrant.

3. Next, whisk in the miso, coconut milk and vegetable stock and bring to the boil. Add the noodles, cover with a lid and cook for 8–10 minutes or until the noodles are just cooked.

4. Stir through the spinach and tofu, then divide the between bowls, add the lime juice and scatter over the zest.

Serves 2
Time 30 minutes

Crispy, crunchy, hearty and super simple, this tray bake is the ideal recipe when you want something satisfying without lots of prep, mess or brain space! The zesty harissa yoghurt is really versatile too; it makes for a great dip or dressing with any veg.

3 floury potatoes, such as
   Maris Piper (about 350g),
   with their skin
½ tablespoon olive oil
2 red onions, halved and finely
   sliced
2 teaspoons paprika
1 punnet of cherry tomatoes
   (about 200g)
1 × 400g tin of butter beans,
   drained
½ bunch of coriander (about
   10–15g), roughly chopped
sea salt

FOR THE HARISSA YOGHURT
4 tablespoons coconut
   yoghurt
2 tablespoons harissa
grated zest and juice of
   2 limes, plus wedges to
   serve

CRISPY POTATO AND PAPRIKA TRAY BAKE

1. Preheat the oven to 220°C fan and bring a large saucepan of salted water to the boil.

2. Cut the potatoes into 1cm cubes then add them to the boiling water. Meanwhile put the olive oil into a large flat baking tray and place in the oven to heat up. Simmer the potatoes for 5 minutes, until softened slightly and a knife pierces them easily, then drain well and add them to the preheated tray along with the onion, paprika and a pinch of sea salt. Toss to combine, then bake for 20 minutes, tossing occasionally so that the potatoes cook evenly.

3. Add the cherry tomatoes and butter beans to the tray and cook for a further 5 minutes until the tomatoes are soft and the potatoes are crisp.

4. Meanwhile make the harissa yoghurt by mixing the coconut yoghurt, harissa, lime zest and juice together in a small bowl, seasoning with salt to taste, then transfer to a small serving bowl.

5. Once the potatoes are ready, remove from the oven, sprinkle over the coriander and serve with the harissa yoghurt on the side.

Serves 2
Time 20 minutes

This is another of my go-to recipes at home; I've been making it for years but come back to it time and again. The miso adds great depth, the yoghurt makes it super creamy and the mix of sage and thyme gives it a lovely freshness.

2 servings of short pasta, such as casarecce, fusilli or farfalle (about 75g per person)
1 tablespoon olive oil
1 onion, thinly sliced
4 garlic cloves, thinly sliced
handful of thyme sprigs (about 5g), leaves picked
handful of sage leaves (about 5g), thinly sliced
400g mushrooms (I love a mixture of chestnut and shiitake), sliced
2 teaspoons brown rice miso paste
4 tablespoons coconut yoghurt
2 large handfuls of spinach, (about 100g), sliced
juice of ½ lemon
sea salt and black pepper

PAN-FRIED SAGE AND MUSHROOM PASTA

1. First, put the pasta on to cook. Bring a large saucepan of salted water to the boil and add the pasta. Cook according to the instructions on the pack or until al dente, then drain, reserving a cupful of the cooking water.

2. While the pasta cooks, place a large frying pan on a medium–low heat and add the olive oil. Once the oil is hot, add the onion and a pinch of salt and cook for about 5 minutes, until softened. Add the garlic, thyme and sage and cook for 2–3 minutes, until fragrant. Pick out a couple of sage leaves and leave to one side, for serving.

3. Increase the heat under the frying pan and add the mushrooms and miso to the onion and herb mix. Cook for 8–10 minutes, stirring frequently, until the mushrooms are golden.

4. Reduce the heat to low, then add the coconut yoghurt, spinach and lemon juice. Toss the drained pasta through the sauce. Add about 100ml of the reserved cooking water. Season generously with salt and pepper and stir it all together for a minute or so, until you have a smooth, creamy sauce.

5. To serve, divide the pasta between serving bowls, add the reserved fried sage and lots of pepper.

'Be sure to use a blender
here, not a food processor,
as that will ensure the
sauce is super smooth.'

Serves 2
Time 15 minutes

I make a variation of this for my kids a lot, using whatever greens I have in the fridge – green beans, asparagus, spinach etc. It's exceptionally simple yet super satisfying.

2 servings of pasta; I like
    orecchiette in this dish
    (about 75g per person)
1 small head broccoli (about
    300g) cut into small florets
100g frozen peas
large handful of cashews
    (about 50g, see Note below)
1 vegetable stock cube
1 teaspoon Dijon mustard
1 tablespoon nutritional yeast
grated zest and juice of
    2 lemons
1 × 400g tin of butter beans,
    drained and rinsed
sea salt and black pepper

LEMONY PEA AND BROCCOLI PASTA

1. Bring a large saucepan of salted water to the boil and add the pasta. Cook according to the instructions on the pack, adding the broccoli and frozen peas for the last 3 minutes of the cooking time. Cook until the pasta is al dente, the broccoli is tender, and the peas are defrosted, then drain and return to the pan.

2. Meanwhile, put the cashews and stock cube into a bowl with 100ml boiling water, let the stock cube dissolve and the cashews soak for 5 minutes.

3. Put the mustard, nutritional yeast, the juice of both lemons and half the zest, and half the tin of butter beans into a high-speed blender along with the cashews and their soaking liquid. Blend until you have a smooth, creamy sauce. Season with salt and pepper to taste.

4. Pour the sauce over the drained pasta and veg, adding the last half of the butter beans. Stir to combine and top with a little extra lemon zest.

NOTE
To make this nut-free,
swap the cashews for
sunflower seeds.

Serves 2
Time 30 minutes

This is exactly the sort of recipe you need on a Monday night; it's super easy, packed with flavour and wonderfully nourishing. I like the mix of flavours and textures here – the gentle spice of the simmered beans, the creamy slices of avocado, the nuttiness of the quinoa and the zest from the lime.

100g quinoa (you could also use pearl barley, rice or bulgur wheat)
2 tablespoons olive oil, plus extra to serve
4 garlic cloves, crushed
1 teaspoon brown rice miso paste
1 tablespoon harissa
1 × 400g tin of black beans
large handful of spinach (about 50g)
1 tablespoon sesame seeds
1 large avocado, thinly sliced
2 limes, the grated zest and juice of 1, the other cut into wedges
1 teaspoon chilli flakes
sea salt and black pepper

SPICY BLACK BEAN, QUINOA AND AVOCADO BOWLS

1. Tip the quinoa into a small saucepan, along with 200ml water and a big pinch of salt. Bring to the boil, then cover with a lid and simmer for 10 minutes, until just cooked. Remove the pan from the heat and set aside until everything else is ready.

2. While the quinoa is cooking, warm a tablespoon of the olive oil in a saucepan set over a medium heat. Add the garlic, miso and harissa and cook for 1–2 minutes, stirring frequently, until the garlic smells fragrant.

3. Add the black beans, along with the water from the tin, and season generously with salt and pepper. Bring to the boil, then cover with a lid and simmer for 20–25 minutes, until any liquid has reduced by half. Add the spinach and stir until it has wilted.

4. While the beans are cooking, toast the sesame seeds in a dry frying pan set over a medium heat, for 2–3 minutes, until golden and fragrant, then remove from the pan and set aside.

5. To serve, fluff the quinoa through with a fork, stir through a little olive oil and divide between serving bowls. Next, add the spicy black beans and avocado. Squeeze the lime juice over the avocado and season with a little salt. Scatter the toasted sesame seeds, chilli flakes and lime zest over the quinoa and serve with a wedge of lime.

Serves 2
Time 30 minutes

Miso aubergines are a staple for every vegetarian, I think. The kick of ginger with miso, maple syrup and rice vinegar gives them brilliant flavour here. They're then served on a bed of lentils, kale, toasted seeds and chives, to keep the meal feeling fresh and light.

small chunk of ginger (about 30g/3cm), peeled and grated or finely chopped

4 tablespoons olive oil, plus extra to serve

4 tablespoons white miso paste

4 tablespoons maple syrup

4 tablespoons brown rice vinegar

2 large aubergines, cut lengthways into eight wedges

1 × 400g tin of brown lentils, drained and rinsed

2 handfuls of mixed seeds, (about 60g); I love a mixture of sesame, pumpkin and sunflower

2 large handfuls of kale (about 100g), tough stalks removed, cut into bite-sized pieces

½ bunch of chives (about 10–15g), finely chopped

pinch of dried chilli flakes

sea salt and black pepper

'To make the aubergine extra sticky, hold back a quarter of the dressing and add it five minutes before the end of the cooking time.'

STICKY MISO AUBERGINES WITH CRUNCHY SEEDS

1. Preheat the oven to 180°C fan and line a large baking tray with baking paper. Then make the sticky miso sauce. Simply add the ginger, 3 tablespoons of the olive oil, the miso, maple syrup and brown rice vinegar to a small bowl and stir until smooth.

2. Place the aubergine on the lined baking tray, season with salt and pour over two thirds of the miso sauce. Toss together so that the aubergine wedges are evenly covered and spread out in a single layer. Roast for 25 minutes, stirring once, until tender.

3. Add the lentils to a second baking tray, drizzle with a tablespoon or so of olive oil, season with salt and pepper and put the tray on to the lower shelf of the oven. Cook for 20–25 minutes, until crispy.

4. Toss the seeds and kale with the remaining dressing and add to the lentil tray for the last 5–10 minutes, until the kale is crisp.

5. Spread the kale and seeds out on a serving platter, then top with the aubergine wedges, crispy lentils, chives, chilli flakes, salt and an extra drizzle of olive oil.

Serves 2
Time 30 minutes

Like a veggie fish and chips, or nuggets and chips, these crispy tofu goujons with pesto mash (made with the potato skin on) are a big hit at home and something I make a lot for my kids (and myself). Dunking the crispy tofu sticks into a little bowl of pesto is delicious! I love this served with a nice peppery salad to balance out the flavours and textures.

3 tablespoons plain white flour
50g panko breadcrumbs
1 teaspoon dried mixed herbs
1 × block of firm tofu (about 300g), drained and cut into 12 sticks
3 tablespoons olive oil
sea salt and black pepper

FOR THE PESTO MASH
400g floury potatoes (such as Maris Piper or King Edward), skin on, cut into large chunks
3 tablespoons oat milk
3 tablespoons olive oil
2 tablespoons basil pesto

'Keeping the skin on the mash saves time and adds extra goodness (there are lots of vitamins and fibre in potato skins), but if you prefer a smooth mash then simply peel the potatoes before you boil them.'

CRISPY TOFU GOUJONS WITH PESTO MASH

1. Put the potatoes into a saucepan of cold salted water, bring to the boil then turn the heat down and simmer on a medium heat for 20 minutes, until tender. Once cooked, drain in a colander and leave to steam for a few minutes.

2. While the potatoes are cooking make the tofu sticks. Add the flour to a shallow bowl and gradually whisk in 75ml water, until you have a smooth, thin paste. Pour the breadcrumbs into a separate shallow bowl, then mix in the dried herbs, a big pinch of salt and a large crack of pepper.

3. Season the tofu sticks on all sides with a little salt, then dip them in the paste one by one, shaking off any excess mixture, then roll in the breadcrumbs until they're evenly coated. You might find it easier (and less messy) to use one hand to dip the sticks into the flour paste, and the other to dip them in the breadcrumbs.

4. Warm a large frying pan over medium–low heat and add the olive oil. Add the tofu sticks to the frying pan and cook for 3–4 minutes on each side, until deeply golden and crispy all over. Keep an eye on the heat – you don't want it too high or the breadcrumbs will cook too quickly and won't brown evenly. Make sure they're not on top of each other either; each one needs space or they won't crisp up.

5. Mash the cooked potatoes, then beat in the oat milk, olive oil and pesto until creamy. Season to taste with salt and pepper and warm over a low heat until hot.

Serves 2
Time 25 minutes

You've got to make both the miso tahini dressing and the toasted herby almonds in this recipe – they're unbelievably delicious and very versatile and I've been adding them to all my salads! The base of the salad can be mixed up though; essentially you want three greens and a grain, but anything from giant couscous and quinoa to fennel, Tenderstem broccoli and asparagus would work brilliantly.

100g pearl barley

200g green beans, trimmed

2 celery stalks, thinly sliced, keep aside any leaves

1 Granny Smith apple, cut into matchsticks

sea salt and black pepper

FOR THE MISO TAHINI DRESSING

1 tablespoon white miso paste

1 tablespoon tahini

1 tablespoon apple cider vinegar

1 tablespoon maple syrup

½ garlic clove, crushed

FOR THE HERBY TOASTED ALMONDS

2 handfuls of almonds (about 60g)

½ garlic clove, crushed

½ bunch of chives (about 10–15g), finely chopped

2 tablespoons olive oil

GARLICKY BARLEY AND GREEN BEAN SALAD WITH HERBY ALMONDS

1. Pour the barley into a saucepan, cover with water and add a big pinch of salt. Bring to the boil, then reduce the heat and simmer for 20 minutes. At this point, add the green beans and cook for a further 3–5 minutes, until the beans and barley are just cooked. Drain and refresh under cold water; give the colander a really good shake to dry everything off.

2. While the barley is cooking, make the dressing. Simply whisk together all the ingredients with a tablespoon of water. You can do this in the bowl that you're serving the salad in to save on washing up.

3. Next, warm a small frying pan over a medium heat. Add the almonds and toast for 6–8 minutes, stirring frequently, until golden. Roughly chop them, then mix them with the garlic, chives, olive oil and a pinch of salt in a small bowl.

4. Add the barley, green beans, celery and apple to the serving bowl. Toss with the dressing and season to taste. Divide between plates, scatter over the celery leaves (if using) and spoon over the herby toasted almonds to finish.

Serves 2
Time 30 minutes

This feels like a Deliciously Ella classic, it's exactly the sort of recipe that made me fall in love with simple, plant-based cooking over 10 years ago and would have fitted into one of my first books perfectly! It's got all my favourite ingredients – sweet potatoes, butter beans, kale and Dijon mustard – and comes together with very minimal prep. The cayenne gives it a nice kick too. This is the sort of recipe I can eat time and again.

2 carrots, roughly chopped
    into large bite-sized chunks
1 large sweet potato (about
    250g), roughly chopped into
    bite-sized chunks
1 small cauliflower, cut into
    florets, leaves removed and
    shredded
1 × 400g tin of butter beans,
    drained and rinsed
1 teaspoon paprika
pinch of cayenne pepper
2 tablespoons olive oil
large handful of kale (about
    50g), tough stalks removed,
    shredded
sea salt and black pepper

FOR THE DRESSING
1 tablespoon olive oil
juice of 1 lemon
1 teaspoon Dijon mustard
1 teaspoon maple syrup
pinch of cayenne pepper

EVERYDAY VEGGIE TRAY BAKE WITH MUSTARD AND CAYENNE PEPPER

1. Preheat the oven to 200°C fan. Place the carrot, sweet potato, cauliflower florets and butter beans on to a large baking tray, sprinkle over the paprika, cayenne and salt, then drizzle with a tablespoon or so of olive oil. Toss everything so that it's all well coated, then roast for 20–25 minutes, until the vegetables are golden and tender.

2. While the veg cook, drizzle another tablespoon of olive oil over the kale and cauliflower leaves in a bowl, massaging the oil into the leaves. Once the roast vegetables are 5 minutes away from being ready, put the leaves on top of the veg and roast for a final 5 minutes, until the kale is crisp.

3. Meanwhile, make the dressing. Simply whisk everything together, seasoning with salt and pepper to taste.

4. Take the tray out of the oven, pour about half the dressing over the veg and mix well. Then divide between two bowls and drizzle the remaining dressing over the top of each to finish.

Serves 2
Time 30 minutes

This bake feels like a shortcut version of cauliflower cheese and it's as creamy, comforting and cosy as it comes. The smooth sauce coats the veg, the thyme adds a lovely herby touch and the crispy pieces of torn sourdough on the top are addictive! Trust me, this will be a firm favourite immediately.

2 large handfuls of cashews (about 100g)
1 cauliflower (about 600g), cut into very small florets
2 leeks (about 500g), tough outer layer removed and thinly sliced
3 tablespoons olive oil, plus extra to serve
400ml oat milk
1½ tablespoons wholegrain mustard
4 tablespoons nutritional yeast
1 vegetable stock cube
3 slices of sourdough (about 150g), torn into small pieces
small handful of thyme (about 5g), leaves picked
1 × 400g tin of butter beans, drained and rinsed
sea salt and black pepper

CRISPY CAULIFLOWER AND THYME BAKE

1. Preheat the oven to 220°C fan. Soak the cashews in boiling water for 5 minutes.

2. Add the cauliflower, leeks and 2 tablespoons of the olive oil to a large baking tray. Season generously with salt and pepper and toss together. Roast in the oven for 15 minutes, stirring halfway, until tender and charred at the edges.

3. Put the oat milk, mustard, nutritional yeast, stock cube, a pinch of salt and lots of pepper into a high-speed blender, along with the drained cashews, and blitz until completely smooth. Taste to check the seasoning and adjust as needed.

4. In a bowl, toss the sourdough with the remaining tablespoon of olive oil, the thyme leaves, a pinch of salt and plenty of pepper.

5. Once the vegetables are ready, remove the tray from the oven and reduce the heat to 210°C fan. Scoop the veg into a smaller ovenproof dish – roughly 28 × 20cm – then add the butter beans and sauce and stir everything together. Scatter over the sourdough and finish with a drizzle of olive oil. Bake for 10 minutes, until bubbling and golden.

'This does make two quite generous portions, so if you don't eat it all then the leftovers keep well. I re-heat it by covering the dish with foil and cooking at 200°C fan, until it's hot and bubbling.'

Serves 2
Time 15 minutes

We all know the feeling of being too tired to cook, when our to-do list feels endless and we want to cut corners – there's a temptation to skip the healthy option when we need it the most. This is the sort of recipe that I turn to on those days; even a takeaway won't arrive quicker than you can get this on the table and the butter bean mash with pan-fried greens and crunchy, garlicky almonds will help give you the energy you need to feel your best.

1 × 400g tin of butter beans
grated zest and juice of
⅟₂ lemon
2 tablespoons olive oil
2 garlic cloves, thinly sliced
½ teaspoon dried chilli flakes
2 handfuls of almonds (about
60g), roughly chopped
½ bunch of flat-leaf parsley
(about 10–15g)
150g Tenderstem broccoli
150g asparagus
sea salt and black pepper

BUTTER BEAN MASH WITH GARLICKY ALMONDS AND GREENS

1. Put the butter beans along with the liquid from the tin into a high-speed blender and blitz until smooth. Season to taste with salt, pepper and the lemon juice.

2. Warm the olive oil in a frying pan set over a low heat. Add the garlic, chilli and almonds and cook for 5 minutes, stirring frequently, until the garlic is golden. Remove the pan from the heat and scoop the garlic, chilli and almonds into a small bowl, leaving the oil in the pan. Stir in the parsley, lemon zest and a pinch of salt and set aside.

3. Set the pan back over a medium–high heat and warm the oil that was left in the pan. Add the broccoli and asparagus and cook for 5 minutes, until tender and lightly charred. To do this, let the vegetables sit undisturbed on the pan for 30 seconds or so, then stir and repeat.

4. To serve, spoon the butter bean mash into serving bowls and smooth into an even layer. Add the charred veg, scatter over the garlicky almonds and chilli and finish with a little salt and pepper.

———

NOTE
You can use any greens here; you just want them to have a gentle bite to maintain a contrast with the soft, creamy mash.

CHAPTER 4

COOK ONCE, EAT TWICE

This chapter is about the small changes and simple habits that make life easier for your future self; asking yourself what can I do today that makes life easier tomorrow? These recipes give you a delicious dinner for tonight, while also doubling up as lunch the next day or helping you stock the freezer so that you have a two-minute dinner later in the week. They're the embodiment of healthy made simple and are what I live by.

Serves 4
Time 30 minutes

On the days that you're tired, lacking in motivation and not wanting to cook, this soup is your best friend. It essentially cooks itself; there's just five minutes of prep at the start. It's deliciously smooth and creamy, packed with goodness and is wonderfully nourishing. The leftovers also freeze brilliantly or make for a great two-minute lunch the next day.

600ml vegetable stock
1 × 400ml tin of coconut milk
2 large sweet potatoes (about 500g), peeled and cut into bite-sized chunks
3 carrots (about 200g), peeled and cut into bite-sized chunks
1 × 400g tin of butter beans
2 garlic cloves, sliced
1 onion, roughly chopped
1 red chilli, halved and deseeded
4 tablespoons coconut yoghurt
sea salt and black pepper
crusty bread, to serve

EVERYDAY BUTTER BEAN, CARROT AND SWEET POTATO SOUP

1. Put the vegetable stock and coconut milk into a large saucepan over a medium heat, bring to the boil, then add the sweet potato, carrot, butter beans, garlic, onion and half the chilli. Put the lid on, turn the heat down to a simmer and cook for 20 minutes, until everything is soft.

2. Either use a stick blender or transfer the soup to a normal blender (make sure it's not boiling at this point as that can break the blender!) and blitz until smooth, seasoning with salt and lots of pepper.

3. Finely slice the other chilli half, then spoon the soup into bowls, swirl through the coconut yoghurt, sprinkle over the red chilli slices and add a little salt, along with a big crack of pepper.

'You can swap the sweet potato for more carrots, pumpkin or any variety of squash depending on what you have in the fridge.'

Serves 4
Time 20 minutes

This nourishing green soup is exactly what you need at the end of a long day. The walnuts and peas add protein and healthy fats, while also giving it delicious flavour, alongside the fresh chives, leeks and garlic. You can serve it as it is, but adding the crunchy, herby crouton mix on the top finishes it off perfectly, adding another layer of flavour and texture. If you're feeling lazy, skip the topping and simply serve with crusty sourdough.

2 tablespoons olive oil
2 leeks, sliced
2 garlic cloves, finely chopped
1 bay leaf
1 head of broccoli (about 400g), cut into small florets, stalk thinly sliced
150g frozen peas
handful of walnuts (about 30g)
1.2 litres hot vegetable stock
½ bunch of chives (about 10–15g), roughly chopped
sea salt and black pepper

FOR THE HERBY CROUTON MIX
handful of pumpkin seeds (about 30g)
handful of walnuts (about 30g)
2 slices of sourdough, cut into small cubes
1 tablespoon olive oil
½ bunch of chives (about 10–15g), finely chopped
pinch of dried chilli flakes

'If you want to mix it up, the leeks can be swapped for onions or shallots, the chives for mint or flat-leaf parsley, and the walnuts for almonds.'

PEA, BROCCOLI AND WALNUT SOUP WITH HERBY CROUTONS

1. Preheat the oven to 180°C fan, then start by making the herby crouton mix. Put the pumpkin seeds, walnuts and sourdough on to a baking tray and drizzle over the olive oil. Bake in the oven for 8–10 minutes, stirring once, until golden. Pour into a bowl and once cool, stir through the chives, chilli flakes and a pinch of salt.

2. While the croutons cook, make the soup. Warm the olive oil in a large saucepan set over a medium heat. Add the leeks, garlic and bay leaf and cook for 10 minutes, stirring often, until softened but not coloured.

3. Next, add the broccoli, peas, walnuts and vegetable stock to the pan, making sure that the broccoli is fully covered. Bring to the boil, then reduce the heat slightly and cook for 4–5 minutes, until the broccoli is cooked but still has a bite.

4. Remove the pan from the heat and fish out the bay leaf, then blitz until smooth using a stick blender or pour into a high-speed blender.

5. Season the soup with salt and pepper to taste. Divide between bowls and spoon over the crunchy crouton topping.

Serves 4
Time 30 minutes

This simple mushroom and lentil soup with salty soy sauce (or tamari), garlic and spinach is light, nutritious and a great batch cook. I take this to work for lunch a lot, either in a Thermos or I'll quickly pop it in the microwave. The swirl of lemony basil pesto on this dish really finishes it off perfectly, adding a nice pop of green too.

2 tablespoons olive oil, plus
    extra to serve
2 onions, finely diced
2 celery stalks, diced
3 garlic cloves, thinly sliced or
    grated
125g mushrooms (I use button
    or chestnut but any work),
    sliced
2 × 400g tins of brown lentils,
    rinsed
1 litre hot vegetable stock
1–2 teaspoons soy sauce or
    tamari
4 tablespoons basil pesto
juice of ½ lemon
3 large handfuls of baby
    spinach (about 150g),
    roughly chopped
sea salt and black pepper

NOURISHING LENTIL, MUSHROOM AND PESTO SOUP

1. Warm the olive oil in a large saucepan set over a medium–low heat. Add the onion, celery, garlic and a big pinch of salt and cook for 10 minutes, until everything has softened (but not browned), stirring every so often to make sure the vegetables don't stick.

2. Increase the heat, then add the mushrooms and cook for 5 minutes, until tender.

3. Add the lentils, hot stock, soy sauce/tamari and season to taste with salt and pepper. Bring to the boil, then reduce the heat slightly and cook for 10 minutes, until the liquid has reduced by a third.

4. Meanwhile, in a small bowl mix together the pesto, lemon juice and a drizzle of olive oil to form a loose sauce.

5. Stir the spinach into the soup until wilted, then divide the soup between bowls and drizzle over the pesto mixture.

NOTE
Add a sprinkling of dried
chilli flakes if you like a hint
of gentle spice.

'You can swap the greens for any other leafy green that's in season, such as spinach, kale or cabbage.'

Serves 4
Time 30 minutes

This chunky, veggie-packed soup is essentially a hot bowl of comforting deliciousness. With five different veggies, plus the white beans, it really is packed with goodness. It's my ideal midweek supper, and the leftovers taste even better, as the flavours really lift the longer it marinates.

2 tablespoons olive oil, plus
    extra to serve
2 onions, diced
2 carrots, diced
2 celery stalks, diced
3 garlic cloves, thinly sliced or
    grated
1 bay leaf
1 × 400g tin of chopped
    tomatoes
2 × 400g tins of white beans
    (you can use butter beans,
    cannellini or haricot beans)
1 vegetable stock cube
4 large handfuls of spring
    greens (about 200g), sliced
    (you can also use kale,
    spinach, cavolo nero or
    cabbage)
sea salt and black pepper

FOR THE GARLIC CROUTONS
2 thick slices of sourdough
1 large garlic clove, peeled
1 teaspoon olive oil
handful of pine nuts (about
    30g)

CHUNKY WHITE BEAN AND VEGGIE SOUP WITH GARLIC CROUTONS

1. Warm the olive oil in a large saucepan set over a medium heat. Add the onion, carrot, celery and a pinch of salt and cook for 10 minutes, until softened but not coloured. Add the garlic and cook for 2–3 minutes, until fragrant.

2. Next add the bay leaf, chopped tomatoes, beans, plus the liquid from their tins, along with 800ml of boiling water. Season well with salt and pepper. Bring to the boil, then reduce the heat a little and cook for 10 minutes or until the liquid has reduced by about a quarter.

3. To make the garlic croutons, toast the sourdough and rub the garlic clove into both sides, then tear each slice into bite-sized pieces. Set a frying pan over a medium heat, then add the sourdough, pine nuts and olive oil. Cook for 4–5 minutes, until golden, and season with salt and pepper.

4. Remove the soup from the heat and using a potato masher, roughly mash about a third of the white beans – this will thicken the soup. Return the pan to a low heat, add the spring greens, then cover with a lid and cook for a few minutes, until the greens are tender.

5. Spoon the soup into bowls and top with the garlic croutons, a drizzle of olive oil and some pepper.

I've been making a variation of lentil bolognese for a good decade now; it's my go-to freezer filler and a quick midweek meal. My original version took too long to prepare in the evenings, so I started making this 'shortcut' version. I use a jar of tomato sauce for instant flavour, mashed chickpeas to make it chunkier and heartier (and to add more goodness as I'm forever looking at ways to get more variety into our diets) and miso for extra depth. I serve it with pasta, jacket potatoes or a grain – either rice, barley or quinoa – and often add a simple green salad on the side too.

2 tablespoons olive oil

1 onion, diced

2 celery stalks, diced

2 medium carrots, diced

2 garlic cloves, crushed or grated

1 × 400g tin of chickpeas, drained and rinsed

1 × 400g tin of green lentils, drained and rinsed

1 × 350g jar of tomato sauce (either tomato and basil, arrabiata or roasted garlic)

300ml hot vegetable stock

1 tablespoon brown rice miso paste

1 teaspoon maple syrup

juice of ½ lemon

sea salt and black pepper

pasta, grain or jacket potatoes, to serve

MY SHORTCUT LENTIL BOLOGNESE

1. Place a sauté pan or shallow casserole dish on a medium heat and add the olive oil. Once the oil is warm, add the onion, celery, carrot and a big pinch of salt. Cook for 10 minutes, until softened, then add the garlic for a further minute.

2. Add the chickpeas, lentils, tomato sauce, stock, miso and maple syrup. Bring to the boil, then reduce to a simmer and cook for 10 minutes, until most of the liquid has reduced and the vegetables are tender.

3. Remove the pan from the heat and gently mash the sauce with a potato masher or fork. You want the chickpeas to end up about the same size as the lentils and the sauce to feel thick enough to coat pasta or fill a jacket potato.

4. Stir through the lemon juice and season to taste. Serve with your choice of pasta/grain/jacket potato.

———

NOTE
I use this for the girls' packed lunches a lot. I make the recipe in a larger batch then just stir a serving through some pasta and pop it in a thermal container.

'To reheat, simply place the leftovers into a saucepan over a medium–low heat, stirring frequently so that it doesn't catch. You might need to add a splash of hot water if it feels too thick. Stir until warmed through.'

Serves 4
Time 30 minutes

This is my husband's favourite recipe in this book. The simple family staple comes together in no time without any fuss. Orzo recipes are a brilliant swap for a risotto – they've got that same creamy texture but are much quicker to make and don't require all the extra stirring, making them the perfect recipe for busy weeks. This dish is best in the summer when the tomatoes are extra juicy and bursting with flavour.

1 tablespoon olive oil

2 shallots or 1 onion

4 garlic cloves, crushed

2 punnets of cherry tomatoes (about 400g), halved

300g orzo

300ml hot vegetable stock

1 × 400g tin of plum tomatoes

1 × 400ml tin of coconut milk

1 × 400g tin of butter beans, drained and rinsed

grated zest and juice of 1 juicy lemon

1 teaspoon maple syrup

2 bunches of basil (about 50g), leaves picked and roughly torn

sea salt and black pepper

SIMPLE TOMATO AND BASIL ORZO

1. Set a medium frying pan over a medium heat, add the olive oil, and cook the shallots, stirring them every so often for 5 minutes, until they start to soften.

2. Add the garlic and cherry tomatoes, and cook for a further 2 minutes, before pouring in the orzo, stock, plum tomatoes and coconut milk. Gently break the plum tomatoes up with the back of a wooden spoon, then bring the mixture to the boil, before reducing to a simmer and cooking for 15–17 minutes. The orzo should be cooked and the dish should feel deliciously creamy with any excess liquid absorbed.

3. Add the butter beans and let them warm through in the sauce for 2 minutes, then add the lemon zest and juice, maple syrup and basil for a final minute, before seasoning with lots of salt and pepper.

'This is a great one for batch cooking and the leftovers are delicious – just loosen the orzo with a little vegetable stock as you reheat it (either in the microwave or on the stove).'

Serves 4
Time 30 minutes

This is a brilliantly zingy recipe with a real kick from the chillies and ginger, a hefty dose of lime and a lovely freshness from the coriander. It's also exceptionally easy to make – all you have to do is chop mushrooms, peel onion and garlic, and that's it! It almost feels like cheating, it tastes so good and is packed with goodness.

1 tablespoon olive oil
400g mixed mushrooms, thinly
   sliced
1 × 400ml tin of coconut milk
200g frozen peas
1 × 400g tin of chickpeas,
   drained and rinsed
sea salt and black pepper

FOR THE CURRY PASTE
2 bunches of coriander (about
   50g)
large chunk of ginger (about
   80g/8cm), peeled and
   chopped
2 garlic cloves, peeled
2 shallots, peeled
2 green jalapeño chillies
2 limes, grated zest of 1, juice
   of 2
50ml water

TO SERVE
1 lime, cut into wedges

EASY PEA-SY CURRY

1. Add the olive oil to a deep frying pan set over a medium-high heat. Add the mushrooms with a pinch of salt and cook for 5 minutes, until tender.

2. While the mushrooms cook, make the curry paste by placing all the ingredients in a food processor with some salt and pepper and blend until a coarse paste forms (I use a mini chopper – it is much smaller and easier to use than a big food processor).

3. Once the mushrooms are soft, add the curry paste to the pan, cooking and stirring for a further 2 minutes before pouring in the coconut milk and chickpeas. Bring the curry to the boil, then turn the heat down to a simmer and cook for 10–15 minutes, until reduced by about a third.

4. Add the peas to the curry for the last 2 minutes, then season to taste and serve with a lime wedge.

'You could use any quick-cook vegetables or protein in here instead of the ones suggested. It's delicious with tofu, bok choi or other greens, and edamame. Root veggies take much longer to cook, so I'd skip those ones.'

Serves 4
Time 30 minutes

This has become my go-to when I'm cooking for friends and family. It's always a real hit and you get maximum flavour for minimal effort. I pop all of the ingredients into a mini chopper and blitz them so that they're incredibly finely chopped and really coat the spaghetti in a beautiful ragu-style sauce.

100g walnuts, finely chopped

1 tablespoon olive oil

1 onion, blitzed in a mini chopper or very finely chopped

2 aubergines, blitzed in a mini chopper or very finely chopped

2 bunches of flat-leaf parsley (about 50g)

4 servings of pasta; I use spaghetti or tagliolini (about 75g per person)

sea salt and pepper

FOR THE PASTE

4 garlic cloves

2 tablespoons harissa

1 red chilli

juice of 1 lemon

1 × 190g jar sun-dried tomatoes (120g drained weight)

SPICY SUN-DRIED TOMATO AND AUBERGINE RAGU

1. Place a frying pan on a high heat and add the walnuts. Toast for about 3 minutes, tossing them a couple of times, then pour them into a small bowl and place to one side.

2. Using the same pan, start the ragu. Pour in the olive oil and warm it over a medium heat, then add the onion and aubergine with some salt and cook for 5 minutes, until they are starting to soften.

3. While they cook, make the paste. Put the garlic, harissa, chilli, sun-dried tomatoes plus 3 tablespoons of olive oil from their jar, and the lemon juice into a mini chopper or food processor and blitz until they form a thick, chunky paste. If you don't have a processor you can finely chop everything and stir it together. Add the sun-dried tomato mix to the aubergine and cook everything together on a low heat for about 10 minutes, until the veg is tender and the sauce is flavoursome.

4. Meanwhile, cook the pasta in boiling salted water, following the instructions on the pack. Once the pasta is cooked, add 150ml of the pasta water to the ragu, and stir until you have a lovely glossy sauce.

5. Stir in the drained pasta, walnuts and parsley, and cook everything together for a minute or so. Season to taste and serve with lots of pepper.

'The aubergine really needs to be cut into 1cm pieces or smaller, or else it won't cook quickly enough and you won't get the same flavours and textures.'

Serves 4
Time 30 minutes

I make this for my family a lot as it's an easy way to pack in loads of greens and the leftovers are brilliant to get a meal on the table in minutes (something I often need to do!). It's a great example of what the book is about; simple ingredients coming together quickly to provide something nutritious and delicious.

2 tablespoons olive oil, plus
    extra to serve
2 leeks, thinly sliced
1 onion, thinly sliced
3 garlic cloves, crushed or
    grated
4 large handfuls of spinach
    (about 200g)
1 × 400ml tin of coconut milk
3 tablespoons basil pesto, plus
    extra to serve
300g orzo
400ml hot vegetable stock
150g frozen peas
grated zest and juice of
    1 lemon
sea salt and black pepper

ONE-PAN SPINACH, LEEK AND PESTO ORZO

1. Place a large saucepan on a medium heat and add the olive oil. Once warm, add the leek, onion, garlic and a big pinch of salt and cook for 10 minutes, until softened but not coloured.

2. Meanwhile, in a blender, blend half the spinach with the coconut milk and pesto to make a smooth, green sauce.

3. Add the orzo to the pan and stir for a minute so that the grains are coated in the cooked veg, before adding the stock and the spinach sauce. Season generously.

4. Bring the liquid back to the boil, then turn the heat down to low, cover with a lid and simmer for 8–10 minutes, stirring it every 5 minutes or so to make sure the orzo doesn't stick to the base of the pan.

5. Roughly slice the remaining spinach and add it to the orzo along with the peas and stir until the spinach has just wilted, then add the lemon zest and juice, season to taste with salt and pepper and serve with a drizzle of olive oil and another spoonful of pesto if you like.

'It's best to add the lemon zest and juice just before serving as this keeps the colour in the sauce more vibrant.'

Serves 4
Time 30 minutes

If you want a simple, hearty recipe this hits the spot every time, plus the leftovers make a perfect packed lunch the next day. I often add sliced avocado, a handful of rocket and a squeeze of lemon with lots of sea salt to my leftovers just to mix it up a little.

1 cauliflower, tough outer leaves discarded, cut into bite-sized florets
2 fennel bulbs, halved lengthways and cut into 1cm wedges, fronds reserved
500g cherry tomatoes
150ml olive oil
1 garlic clove, crushed
grated zest and juice of 1 lemon
½ teaspoon dried thyme
½ teaspoon dried oregano
bunch of basil (about 25g), leaves torn
500g cooked Puy lentils or 2 × 400g tins of green lentils, drained and rinsed
sea salt and black pepper

ROASTED CAULIFLOWER, FENNEL, TOMATO AND PUY LENTIL TRAY BAKE

1. Preheat the oven to 190°C fan.

2. In a medium bowl, toss the cauliflower, fennel, cherry tomatoes, 2 tablespoons of the olive oil, a big pinch of salt and some black pepper, then spread everything out on a large baking tray. The vegetables need to be in a single layer, so that they roast rather than steam, so use two baking trays if you don't have one big enough. Roast in the oven for 25 minutes or until just tender and charred at the edges.

3. To make the dressing, whisk together the remaining 120ml of olive oil, the garlic, lemon zest and juice, thyme, oregano and basil and season to taste with salt and pepper. Stir half the dressing through the lentils and set the rest aside.

4. Once the vegetables are cooked, stir through the lentils, drizzle over the remaining dressing and season to taste with salt and pepper.

'The beauty of this recipe is the flexibility. Swap cauliflower for aubergine, romanesco or broccoli, and use beluga lentils, wild rice or wholegrain freekeh instead of the Puy lentils – basically use what you've got in the house!'

The best thing about batch cooking is that the flavours of the dish tend to get better the longer they marinate, so the leftovers are always a real treat, and this is certainly the case in this recipe. It's hearty and cosy, with lovely spices from the harissa, sweetness from the coconut and maple syrup and a delicious nutty flavour from the almonds. The aubergine gives it great texture, while the beans ensure it really fills you up. It's great on its own for a light supper, or for something a bit more substantial serve it with jasmine rice, jacket potatoes or crispy roast cauliflower (see Note below).

1 tablespoon olive oil
2 shallots, halved and finely sliced
1 aubergine, finely diced into 1cm cubes
4 garlic cloves, crushed
1 × 400g tin of black beans, drained and rinsed
3 tablespoons harissa, plus extra to serve
1 × 400ml tin of coconut milk
400ml hot vegetable stock
2 heaped tablespoons smooth almond butter
2 teaspoons maple syrup
grated zest and juice of 2 juicy limes
sea salt and black pepper

CREAMY BLACK BEAN, HARISSA AND ALMOND BUTTER STEW

1. Put the olive oil into a large frying pan over a medium heat, add the shallot and aubergine and a pinch of salt and fry for 5 minutes, until soft. Add the garlic, black beans and harissa and fry for 2 minutes, until fragrant.

2. Pour in the coconut milk, stock, almond butter and maple syrup. Bring to a boil, then put the lid on the pan and turn the heat down to a simmer. Cook for 15 minutes, until the sauce has thickened.

3. Stir in the lime zest and juice and season with salt and pepper to taste. Swirl an extra tablespoon of harissa through the stew to serve (if you'd like a little extra spice).

___

NOTE
To make crispy roast cauliflower, simply chop your cauliflower into small florets, place them on a baking tray with a tablespoon or so of olive oil and a sprinkling of salt and roast in an oven preheated to 200ºC fan for about 20–25 minutes, until golden and crispy.

'My girls love this recipe too, so when I'm cooking it for the family I hold off on the harissa and stir it into the adult portions once I've served the little ones.'

Serves 4
Time 30 minutes

I first made a similar recipe to this one for Zac Efron for a Netflix show he was working on (a real pinch me moment!) and it went on to be our most popular recipe ever. The original version has almost 20 ingredients though and takes about an hour to cook, so I started making this version and it's become a staple in our house. The chickpeas add protein as well as being one of five different veggies alongside cauliflower, peppers, onion and garlic.

1 cauliflower, cut into bite-sized florets
2 red peppers, deseeded and sliced
2 teaspoons curry powder (mild or medium)
2 tablespoons olive oil
1 red onion, thinly sliced
4 garlic cloves, crushed or finely chopped
2 chillies, thinly sliced
1 × 400ml tin of coconut milk
1 × 400g tin of chickpeas, drained and rinsed
1 tablespoon maple syrup
2 juicy limes, the juice of 1, the other cut into wedges
sea salt and black pepper

EASY CHICKPEA AND VEGGIE CURRY

1. Preheat the oven to 220°C fan. Toss the cauliflower, pepper and curry powder with 1 tablespoon of the olive oil and a big pinch of salt. I find that rubbing the spices into the veggies with my hands is the easiest way to get them evenly coated. Roast for 20–25 minutes, until everything is deeply golden and tender.

2. Meanwhile, place a heavy-based saucepan on a medium heat and add a tablespoon of olive oil. Once hot, add the red onion, garlic and chilli and cook for 10 minutes, until soft and translucent.

3. Next, add the coconut milk, chickpeas and maple syrup, bring to a simmer and cook for 10–15 minutes, or until the roasted vegetables are ready. Remove the vegetables from the oven and stir them into the sauce, add the lime juice and season to taste with salt and pepper.

4. Serve with the remaining lime wedges on the side.

Serves 4
Time 20 minutes

I remember the first time I had a tagine. My husband Matthew and I went to Morocco on a little babymoon just before our first daughter was born in 2019. The flavours were perfect and I came home very excited to recreate something similar. So, here's my simple, at-home take on a veggie tagine – it's a one-pot wonder that's full of flavour and ready in next to no time. I like to serve it with a simple green salad on the side.

2 tablespoons olive oil
2 red onions, cut into small
    wedges
4 carrots, cut into small cubes
2 courgettes, halved and finely
    sliced
2 teaspoons ground cumin
2 teaspoons ground cinnamon
2 × 400g tins of chickpeas,
    drained and rinsed
2 × 400g tins of chopped
    tomatoes
150g dried apricots, roughly
    chopped
700ml vegetable stock
230g giant couscous
2 tablespoons harissa
sea salt and black pepper

SIMPLE VEGGIE AND APRICOT TAGINE

1. Put the olive oil into a large saucepan over a medium heat and add the onion, carrot and courgette and fry for 5 minutes, until the vegetables are just starting to soften and colour slightly.

2. Tip in the cumin and cinnamon and fry for 30 seconds until they smell fragrant. Add the chickpeas, tomatoes, dried apricots and stock and bring to the boil.

3. Stir in the couscous, cover and cook for 8–10 minutes, until the vegetables are soft and the couscous is tender.

4. Stir though the harissa and season to taste with salt and pepper.

Serves 4
Time 30 minutes

This is a versatile curry, so you can use the base recipe alongside whatever you've got in the fridge, from courgettes and mangetout to tofu and chickpeas. It's served topped with crunchy cashews to add delicious texture.

1 tablespoon garam masala

2 tablespoons olive oil

2 onions, thinly sliced

2 garlic cloves, grated or finely chopped

small chunk of ginger (about 30g/3cm), peeled and grated or finely chopped

2–3 bird's eye chillies, thinly sliced

1 × 400ml tin of coconut milk

200g green beans, trimmed

200g frozen peas, defrosted

2 large handfuls of baby spinach (about 100g)

handful of cashews (about 30g)

sea salt and black pepper

GREEN BEAN, SPINACH AND CASHEW CURRY

1. Heat a small frying pan over a medium heat, then add the garam masala and toast for about 30 seconds, until fragrant. Pour into a bowl and set aside.

2. Set a shallow casserole or large frying pan over a medium heat and add the olive oil. Add the onion, garlic, ginger, chilli and a pinch of salt and cook for 10 minutes, stirring frequently, until softened and translucent.

3. Next, add the toasted garam masala, coconut milk, a few big cracks of black pepper and green beans. Half fill the empty coconut milk tin with water and pour it into the pan. Season with salt and bring to the boil, then reduce the heat and simmer for about 8–10 minutes, until the beans are just tender and the liquid has reduced by about half.

4. While the curry is cooking, put the small frying pan back on to a medium–low heat. Add the cashews and cook for 6–8 minutes, tossing frequently, until golden all over. Remove from the pan and roughly chop once they're cool enough to touch.

5. Stir the peas and spinach into the curry and cook until the spinach has wilted and the peas have warmed through. Taste to check the seasoning and adjust as needed. Serve topped with the cashews and extra chilli, if you like more heat.

'For more colour, add a teaspoon of ground turmeric in step 3, when you add the coconut milk and green beans.'

Serves 4
Time 30 minutes

Dhal is one of my go-to recipes when I want something that's equal parts easy, comforting and nourishing. Plus the flavour only gets deeper and better with time, so the leftovers are a huge hit later in the week. Here's a speedy, simple version that always hits the spot.

2 tablespoons olive oil

1 teaspoon cumin seeds

1 bay leaf

2 onions, finely sliced

1–2 red or green chillies, thinly sliced (or 1–2 teaspoons dried chilli flakes)

2 garlic cloves, crushed or grated

small chunk of ginger (about 30g/3cm), peeled and grated

300g red lentils, rinsed

½ teaspoon ground turmeric

juice of 1 lemon

bunch of coriander, leaves picked (about 10–25g, depending on how much you like it!)

sea salt and black pepper

SPEEDY ONE-POT DHAL

1. Warm the olive oil in a large saucepan set over a medium heat. Add the cumin seeds and bay leaf and fry for 30 seconds, until fragrant, then add the onion, chilli, garlic, ginger and a big pinch of salt. Cook for 10 minutes, stirring occasionally, until the onions are soft and translucent.

2. Add the lentils, turmeric and 900ml of boiling water. Bring to the boil, then cover with a lid and simmer for 15–20 minutes, until the lentils are completely tender, stirring occasionally to stop the lentils from catching. Season with salt, to taste.

3. Remove the dhal from the heat and leave to stand for a few minutes then stir in the lemon juice. It's best to add the lemon juice just before serving, so if you're saving half the dish for later, I'd add half the lemon juice now and add the rest just before you eat it (it stores brilliantly for up to five days in the fridge and freezes very well too).

4. Divide the dhal between serving bowls and scatter over the coriander leaves.

Serves 4
Time 30 minutes

This is a great way of getting lots of flavour on the table in no time. Using a jar of peppers with thyme and harissa instantly transforms a handful of simple ingredients into something special.

2 aubergines, cut into 1cm dice

2 courgettes, cut into 1cm dice

4 garlic cloves, grated or finely chopped

1 teaspoon dried thyme or fresh thyme leaves

2 tablespoons olive oil, plus extra to serve

300g orzo

2 tablespoons harissa

1 × 400g tin of cherry tomatoes

1 × 400g tin of butter beans, drained

1 × 300–400g jar of roasted peppers in oil, drained and diced, plus about 2 tablespoons of the oil to serve

2 large handfuls of rocket (about 100g)

sea salt and black pepper

ROASTED PEPPER, THYME AND BUTTER BEAN TRAY BAKE

1. Preheat the oven to 200°C fan. Tip the aubergine, courgette, garlic, thyme and olive oil into a large baking tray. Add a big pinch of salt, stir and roast for 10 minutes.

2. Remove the tray from the oven and add the orzo, harissa, tomatoes, butter beans and roasted peppers. Fill the empty tomato tin with water and pour this in too. Add a big pinch of salt, lots of pepper, stir everything together then level the surface. It's important to season the pasta really well here so that you get maximum flavour.

3. Return the tray to the oven for 18–20 minutes, until the orzo is cooked but still has a bite to it – it will continue to absorb liquid and cook as it cools.

4. To serve, spoon the orzo mixture on to plates, scatter over a handful of rocket and drizzle with a little of the olive oil from the pepper jar.

NOTE
For little ones, swap the harissa for pesto.

Serves 4
Time 30 minutes

The combination of flavours in here is as good as it gets: peanut butter, lime, chilli, ginger and garlic simmered with coconut milk, shallots and cauliflower. The stew is extra creamy so it feels deliciously indulgent, exactly what you need when a bowl of comfort food calls! Adding some extra ginger and chilli at the end gives the stew some additional crunch and a touch more heat if you like that, but it's not needed.

4 servings of rice; I like brown basmati rice (about 50g per person), rinsed
2 tablespoons olive oil
2 shallots, thinly sliced
4 garlic cloves, finely chopped or crushed
small chunk of ginger (about 30g/3cm), peeled and finely chopped or grated, plus some optional extra matchsticks to serve
2–3 red finger chillies, thinly sliced
2 teaspoons curry powder
1 large cauliflower, cut into bite-sized florets
1 × 400g tin of coconut milk
3 heaped tablespoons crunchy peanut butter
1 vegetable stock cube
juice of 1 lime
sea salt and black pepper

ONE-PAN PEANUT AND CAULIFLOWER STEW

1. Tip the rice into a small saucepan and add 500ml of water and a big pinch of salt. Bring to the boil then reduce the heat to low, cover with a lid, and cook for 20–25 minutes, until all the water has been absorbed. Leave to stand for a few minutes before serving.

2. While the rice is cooking, set a large wok or sauté pan over a medium–low heat and add the olive oil. Once warm, add the shallot, garlic, ginger, chilli and a pinch of salt and cook for 10 minutes, until softened and fragrant.

3. Next, add the curry powder and cook for a minute, until fragrant, then stir in the cauliflower.

4. Add the coconut milk, peanut butter, a pinch of salt and crumble in the stock cube. Bring to a simmer, then cover with a lid and cook for 10 minutes, until the cauliflower is just tender. It should be cooked but still with a good crunch to it.

5. Stir in the lime juice and taste to check the seasoning. Spoon into serving bowls, scatter over the ginger matchsticks (if using), and serve with the rice.

'The leftovers are delicious served with pitta bread for lunch or piled into a hot jacket potato for dinner.'

———

NOTE
The colour of the stew might change according to the peanut butter you use – a darker roast will make the stew darker.

Serves 4
Time 30 minutes

I do a lot of batch cooking at home – it's what enables me to give me and my family simple, healthy meals on busy weeks. I'd be lost without my freezer bags of pre-prepped meals and this is one of my go-tos. I started adding tofu and white beans to my pasta sauces so that I could quickly boil a bag of pasta and know that I was serving a nutritious dinner that was packed with protein, fibre, vitamins and minerals.

3 peppers (I love a mixture of red and yellow), thinly sliced

3 courgettes, thinly sliced

2 tablespoons olive oil

2 onions, diced

8 garlic cloves, crushed or finely chopped

1 × 500g jar of passata

1 × 400g tin of cannellini beans, drained

1 vegetable stock cube

1 × 300g block of silken tofu

1½ teaspoons maple syrup

1 teaspoon brown rice miso

sea salt and black pepper

2 servings of pasta (about 75g per person) or your grain of choice, to serve

ROASTED MEDITERRANEAN VEG AND CANNELLINI BEAN TOMATO SAUCE

1. Preheat the oven to 200°C fan. Add the peppers, courgettes and a tablespoon of the olive oil to a large baking tray (you might need to use two if you don't have one large enough to fit the vegetables in a single layer). Season generously with salt and pepper and toss. Cook for 20–25 minutes, stirring halfway, until golden.

2. Next, make the base of the sauce. Warm the remaining tablespoon of olive oil in a saucepan set over a medium heat. Add the onion and cook for 10 minutes, until soft and translucent, adding the garlic for the last couple of minutes.

3. Add the passata, cannellini beans, stock cube and a pinch of salt. Fill the empty passata jar with water and add this too (about 400ml water). Bring to the boil then reduce the heat to medium–low and simmer for 10 minutes, until the liquid has reduced by about a third. At this point cook your pasta or grain in salted boiling water according to the instructions on the pack.

4. Add the tofu, maple syrup and miso to the pan, then use a stick–blender to blitz the sauce, until smooth. Season to taste.

5. Finally, stir in the roasted veg. Serve stirred through your pasta or cooked grains.

'When my kids are being fussy, I either finely chop, blend or roughly mash (with a potato masher) all the veg into the sauce – it means they still get all the goodness without noticing the veg!'

Serves 4 (makes 10
patties)
Time 25 minutes

This is another family favourite in our house; my kids love them and
they're a really handy option for busy weeks. I often double the recipe
so that we have lots to put into lunchboxes (using a no-nut pesto!) or for
me to put on top of simple salads for lunch. You can swap the basil pesto
for harissa or tomato pesto to switch up the flavours.

2 tablespoons milled flaxseed

3 tablespoons olive oil

1 onion, finely chopped

1 garlic clove, crushed

4 heaped tablespoons basil
    pesto

2 tablespoons nutritional yeast
    (optional)

250g cooked quinoa (see Note
    below; 100g raw)

4 heaped tablespoons plain
    flour (70g)

sea salt and black pepper

1 lemon, cut into wedges, to
    serve

PESTO QUINOA FRITTERS

1. If you need to cook your quinoa, cook it at this point
according to the instructions on the pack, allowing plenty
of time for it to cool – if the quinoa is hot and wet, the
fritters won't bind.

2. In a small bowl, combine the milled flaxseed with
50ml water. Set aside to absorb until thickened – about
10 minutes. This acts as a binder in the fritters.

3. While the flaxseed soaks, heat 1 tablespoon of the
olive oil in a large non-stick frying pan over a medium
heat. Add the onion and cook for about 5 minutes, stirring
frequently, until softened, then add the garlic and cook for
another minute. Remove from the heat and set aside to
cool for a couple of minutes.

4. Put the cooked quinoa, pesto, nutritional yeast and
flour into a large bowl. Season generously with salt and
pepper, then stir in the cooked onion mixture and the
soaked flaxseed. Divide the mixture into 10 equal-sized
portions and shape into patties. There's no need to weigh
them, but for reference they're about 35g each.

5. Heat the remaining tablespoon of olive oil in the same
frying pan that you used for the onion over a medium–
low heat. Add roughly half the fritters to the pan and
cook for 3–4 minutes on each side, until golden and crisp.
Be careful not to overcrowd the pan or the fritters won't
brown. Repeat with the remaining fritters, adding another
tablespoon of oil for each batch. Serve with lemon wedges.

NOTE
I find these much easier to
make with bags of pre-cooked
quinoa. If you're cooking the
quinoa from scratch then
make sure it's completely cool
and there's no residual liquid
before making the patties,
otherwise, they'll be too wet.
The fritters still work but won't
go as nice and crispy.

'To store the fritters, let them cool completely then place them in an airtight container in the fridge for up to five days.'

Serves 4
Time 20 minutes

I'm always thinking about different ways to get more veggies into my meals and this recipe is such a great way of upping your greens, with spinach in both the sauce and the broth. It's delicious as a light supper and feels like a mix between a soup, broth and a stew; equally serve it with brown rice or another grain, a toasted piece of sourdough, a jacket potato, roasted veggies or pan-fried greens.

1 tablespoon olive oil
2 shallots, thinly sliced
2 leeks, cut into 1cm slices
4 garlic cloves, finely chopped
1 vegetable stock cube
2 × 400g tins of butter beans
4 large handfuls of spinach
　　(about 200g), roughly
　　chopped
grated zest and juice of
　　1 lemon
sea salt and black pepper

FOR THE SAUCE
100ml oat milk
½ teaspoon brown rice miso
　　paste
2 tablespoons nutritional yeast
large handful of baby spinach
　　(about 50g)

CREAMY LEEK, SPINACH AND BUTTER BEAN BOWLS

1. Set a heavy-bottomed saucepan over a medium heat and add the olive oil. Once the oil is warm, add the shallots, leeks and a pinch of salt. Cook for 8–10 minutes, stirring occasionally, until they soften. Add the garlic and cook for a further 2 minutes, until it's golden and fragrant.

2. Next, add the stock cube and butter beans, along with the liquid from each of the tins. Bring to the boil, then cover with a lid and simmer for 10 minutes, until thickened.

3. While the beans are cooking, make the sauce. Simply put the oat milk, miso, nutritional yeast and the baby spinach into a high-speed blender and blitz until perfectly smooth.

4. Once the beans are ready, pour in the sauce and add the spinach, stirring until it's wilted. Stir in the lemon juice and season to taste with salt and pepper. Scatter over the lemon zest before serving.

'For anyone that grows fresh thyme, definitely add it to this recipe, just add a small handful of picked leaves with the garlic at the start.'

INDEX

Note: page numbers in **bold** refer to illustrations.

almond
    garlicky almonds **138**, 139
    herby toasted almonds **132**, 133
almond butter 21, 24, 72
    creamy black bean, harissa and
        almond butter stew 164, **165**
apple 24, 133
    oaty almond butter and apple bars 37
    walnut, cinnamon and apple
        porridge **20**, 21
apricot and veggie simple tagine 168, **169**
aubergine 108, 164, 175
    herby jewelled rice with roasted
        aubergine, walnuts, mint and
        pomegranate **110**, 111
    spicy sun-dried tomato and aubergine
        ragu **158**, 159
    sticky miso aubergines with crunchy
        seeds **128**, 129
    warm Mediterranean aubergine and
        basil orzo salad **48**, 49
avocado 42, 89, 104
    15-minute herby avocado noodles 82,
        83
    avocado and butter lettuce salad with
        a crunchy protein topping 66, **67–8**
    butter beans, greens and avocado
        toasts 28, **29**
    chopped guacamole-style salad 46
    smashed chickpea guacamole
        sandwich 61
    spicy avocado dressing 46, **47**
    spicy black bean, quinoa and avocado
        bowls 126, **127**

banana 24
    blueberry, banana and peanut
        porridge 21
barley, garlicky barley with green bean
    salad with herby almonds **132**, 133
basil 30, 77, 163
    simple tomato and basil orzo **154**, 155
    sun-dried tomato, basil and olive pasta
        salad **80**, 81
    warm Mediterranean aubergine and
        basil orzo salad **48**, 49
bean(s)
    chunky white bean and veggie soup
        with garlic croutons **148**, 149
    see also black bean; butter bean;
        cannellini bean; green bean

beetroot
    creamy beetroot, lentil and yoghurt
        salad with toasted pitta **64**,
        65
    creamy beetroot, miso and tofu
        noodles **116**, 117
berry
    berry, oats and peanut butter
        smoothie 24, **25**
    blueberry, banana and peanut
        porridge 21
black bean 46, 53
    creamy black bean, harissa and
        almond butter stew 164, **165**
    spicy black bean, quinoa and avocado
        bowls 126, **127**
blenders 13, 15
blueberry, banana and peanut
    porridge 21
bolognese, my shortcut lentil 152, **153**
breakfasts 19–38
broccoli
    garlicky broccoli and chilli protein
        bowls **102**, 103
    lemony pea and broccoli pasta **124**,
        125
    pea, broccoli and walnut soup with
        herby croutons **144**, 145
    see also Tenderstem broccoli
butter bean 121, 125, 134, 136
    butter bean mash with garlicky
        almonds and greens **138**, 139
    butter beans, greens and avocado
        toasts 28, **29**
    chunky white bean and veggie soup
        with garlic croutons **148**, 149
    cosy roasted shallot and butter bean
        bowls 98, **99**
    creamy leek, spinach and butter bean
        bowls **182**, 183
    creamy tahini beans on toast 54, **55**
    everyday butter bean, carrot and
        sweet potato soup 142, **143**
    roasted pepper, thyme and butter
        bean tray bake 175
    simple tomato and basil orzo 155

cabbage 45, 62, 149
    crispy one-tray hispi cabbage with
        garlic yoghurt 108, **109**
cacao powder 21, 38
cannellini bean 28
    chunky white bean and veggie soup
        with garlic croutons **148**, 149

roasted Mediterranean veg and
        cannellini bean tomato sauce **178**,
        179
carbohydrates 14, 15
carrot
    10-minute miso and ginger salad 53
    carrot cake flapjacks 34, **35**
    chunky white bean and veggie soup
        with garlic croutons 149
    crunchy satay potato salad 62
    everyday butter bean, carrot and
        sweet potato soup 142, **143**
    everyday veggie tray bake with
        mustard and cayenne pepper 134
    herby summer rolls 72
    my everyday ginger and chilli stir-
        fry 114
    my shortcut lentil bolognese 152
    simple veggie and apricot tagine
        168
    spicy tofu bowl with crunchy slaw
        45
cashews 77, 125, 136
    creamy cashew dressing **88**, 89
    green bean, spinach and cashew
        curry **170**, 171
cauliflower 134, 167
    crispy cauliflower and thyme
        bake 136, **137**
    one-pan peanut and cauliflower
        stew 176, **177**
    roasted cauliflower, fennel, tomato and
        Puy lentil tray bake **162**, 163
cavolo nero 117, 149
    cavolo nero and walnut spaghetti **92**,
        93
celery 24, 133, 146, 149, 152
chia seed 21, 24
chickpea
    15-minute chickpea, edamame and
        miso stew 86, **87**
    apricot and veggie tagine 168
    avocado and butter lettuce salad with
        a crunchy protein topping 66
    crispy one-tray hispi cabbage with
        garlic yoghurt 108
    easy chickpea and veggie curry **166**,
        167
    easy pea-sy curry 156
    my shortcut lentil Bolognese 152
    smashed chickpea guacamole
        sandwich **60**, 61
    sweet and spicy kale, walnut and
        chickpea salad 42, **43**

chilli
  garlicky broccoli and chilli protein bowls **102**, 103
  mango, mint and chilli sunshine bowls **70**, 71
  my everyday ginger and chilli stir-fry 114, **115**
  slow-cooked courgette, olive oil and chilli linguine 94, **95**
chives 66, 82, 129, 145
chocolate
  chocolate orange porridge **20**, 21
  double chocolate oaty bites 38, **39**
  freezer chocolate chip cookies **32**, 33
choppers, mini pro 13, 15
cinnamon 34, 37, 168
  walnut, cinnamon and apple porridge **20**, 21
coconut milk
  15-minute chickpea, edamame and miso stew 86
  comforting udon noodle bowls with mushroom and coconut 118, **119**
  creamy black bean, harissa and almond butter stew 164
  easy chickpea and veggie curry 167
  easy pea-sy curry 156
  everyday butter bean, carrot and sweet potato soup 142
  green bean, spinach and cashew curry 171
  one-pan peanut and cauliflower stew 176
  simple tomato and basil orzo 155
  smoothies 24
coconut yoghurt
  coriander and ginger yoghurt **96**, 97
  creamy beetroot, lentil and yoghurt salad **64**, 65
  crispy potato and paprika tray bake 121
  everyday butter bean, carrot and sweet potato soup 142
  garlic yoghurt 108, **109**
  herby yoghurt 58, **59**
  pan-fried sage and mushroom pasta 122
  satay sauce 62
cookies, freezer chocolate chip **32**, 33
coriander (fresh)
  15-minute black dhal 85
  chopped guacamole-style salad 46
  coriander and ginger yoghurt 97
  creamy beetroot, lentil and yoghurt salad with toasted pitta 65
  crispy potato and paprika tray bake 121
  crunchy satay potato salad 62
  curry paste 156

herby green sauce 77
herby summer rolls 72
herby yoghurt 58
smashed chickpea guacamole sandwich 61
spicy tofu bowl with crunchy slaw 45
courgette 49, 168, 175, 179
  slow-cooked courgette, olive oil and chilli linguine 94, **95**
couscous, simple veggie and apricot tagine 168
croutons
  garlic **148**, 149
  herby **144**, 145
cucumber
  10-minute miso and ginger salad 53
  crunchy tofu, quinoa and tahini protein bowls 104
  herby summer rolls 72
  mango, mint and chilli sunshine bowls 71
  quick pan-fried tofu and herby yoghurt sandwich 58
  spicy tofu bowl with crunchy slaw 45
  sun-dried tomato, basil and olive pasta salad 81
  super green edamame salad 50
curry
  curry paste 156
  easy chickpea and veggie curry **166**, 167
  easy pea-sy curry 156, **157**
  green bean, spinach and cashew curry **170**, 171
  speedy one-pot dhal 172, **173**

dhal
  15-minute black **84**, 85
  speedy one-pot 172, **173**
dill 65, 77
dipping sauce 72, **73**
dressings 42, 50, 66, 78, 81, 134
  coriander and ginger yoghurt **96**, 97
  creamy cashew **88**, 89
  harissa **110**, 111
  harissa peanut 45
  miso tahini 133
  spicy avocado 46, **47**
  tahini 104, **105**
  teriyaki 53

edamame 14
  10-minute miso and ginger salad 53
  15-minute chickpea, edamame and miso stew 86, **87**
  creamy beetroot, miso and tofu noodles 117
  garlicky broccoli and chilli protein bowls 103

miso mushroom bowls 78
my go-to green pasta 77
super green edamame salad 50, **51**
equipment 13, 15

fats, healthy 14
fennel, roasted cauliflower, fennel, tomato and Puy lentil tray bake **162**, 163
flaxseed
  freezer chocolate chip cookies 33
  oaty almond butter and apple bars 37
  pesto quinoa fritters 180
  prep-ahead porridge 21
  seedy green pesto muffins 30
food groups 14
fritters, pesto quinoa 180, **181**

garlic
  garlic croutons **148**, 149
  garlic yoghurt 108, **109**
  garlicky almonds **138**, 139
  garlicky barley with green bean salad with herby almonds **132**, 133
  garlicky broccoli and chilli protein bowls **102**, 103
ginger
  10-minute miso and ginger salad **52**, 53
  coriander and ginger yoghurt **96**, 97
  how to peel 52
  my everyday ginger and chilli stir-fry 114, **115**
green bean 98, 171
  garlicky barley with green bean salad with herby almonds **132**, 133
guacamole
  chopped guacamole-style salad 46, **47**
  smashed chickpea guacamole sandwich **60**, 61
gut health 15

harissa
  creamy beetroot, lentil and yoghurt salad with toasted pitta 65
  creamy black bean, harissa and almond butter stew 164, **165**
  crispy potato and paprika tray bake 121
  harissa dressing **110**, 111
  harissa peanut dressing 45
  harissa scrambled tofu on toast **56**, 57
  roasted pepper, thyme and butter bean tray bake 175
  simple veggie and apricot tagine 168
  spicy black bean, quinoa and avocado bowls 126
  spicy sun-dried tomato and aubergine ragu 159

hazelnuts 21, 38
healthy lifestyles 14–17
hemp seed 21, 24

kale
    butter beans, greens and avocado
        toasts 28
    chunky white bean and veggie soup
        with garlic croutons 149
    creamy beetroot, miso and tofu
        noodles 117
    everyday veggie tray bake with
        mustard and cayenne pepper 134
    my every single day salad 89
    sticky miso aubergines with crunchy
        seeds 129
    sweet potato and crispy lentil
        bowls with coriander and ginger
        yoghurt 97
    sweet and spicy kale, walnut and
        chickpea salad 42, **43**

leek
    creamy leek, spinach and butter bean
        bowls **182**, 183
    crispy cauliflower and thyme bake 136
    my everyday ginger and chilli stir-
        fry 114
    one-pan spinach, leek and pesto
        orzo 160, **161**
    pea, broccoli and walnut soup with
        herby croutons 145
lemony pea and broccoli pasta **124**, 125
lentils 14
    my shortcut lentil bolognese 152, **153**
lentils (brown)
    nourishing lentil, mushroom and pesto
        soup 146, **147**
    sticky miso aubergines with crunchy
        seeds **128**, 129
lentils (green)
    creamy beetroot, lentil and yoghurt
        salad with toasted pitta **64**, 65
    sweet potato and crispy lentil
        bowls with coriander and ginger
        yoghurt **96**, 97
lentils (Puy)
    15-minute black dhal **84**, 85
    roasted cauliflower, fennel, tomato and
        Puy lentil tray bake **162**, 163
lentil(s) (red), speedy one-pot dhal 172
lettuce 46
    avocado and butter lettuce salad with
        a crunchy protein topping 66,
        67–8
lime, tahini and pea toasts 28, **29**
linguine, slow-cooked courgette, olive oil
    and chilli 94, **95**
lunches 41–89

mango 71
    mango, mint and chilli sunshine
        bowls **70**, 71
    sunshine mango smoothie 24, **25**
mash
    butter bean **138**, 139
    pesto 130, **131**
mint
    herby jewelled rice with roasted
        aubergine, walnuts, mint and
        pomegranate **110**, 111
    mango, mint and chilli sunshine
        bowls **70**, 71
miso (brown rice)
    10-minute miso and ginger salad **52**,
        53
    comforting udon noodle bowls with
        mushroom and coconut 118
    creamy leek, spinach and butter bean
        bowls 183
    miso mushroom bowls 78, **79**
    mushroom, miso and tofu toasts 29,
        29
    my shortcut lentil Bolognese 152
    pan-fried sage and mushroom
        pasta 122
    roasted Mediterranean veg and
        cannellini bean tomato sauce 179
    spicy black bean, quinoa and avocado
        bowls 126
miso (white)
    15-minute chickpea, edamame and
        miso stew 86, **87**
    creamy beetroot, miso and tofu
        noodles **116**, 117
    miso tahini dressing 133
    sticky miso aubergines with crunchy
        seeds **128**, 129
muffins, seedy green pesto 30, **31**
mushroom
    comforting udon noodle bowls with
        mushroom and coconut 118, **119**
    easy pea-sy curry 156
    miso mushroom bowls 78, **79**
    mushroom, miso and tofu toasts 29,
        29
    nourishing lentil, mushroom and pesto
        soup 146, **147**
    pan-fried sage and mushroom
        pasta 122, **123**

noodles (soba)
    15-minute herby avocado noodles 82,
        83
    creamy beetroot, miso and tofu
        noodles **116**, 117
noodles (udon), comforting udon
    noodle bowls with mushroom and
    coconut 118, **119**

noodles (vermicelli), herby summer
    rolls 72
nut butters 15
    see also almond butter
nuts 15
    see also cashews; hazelnut; walnut

oat milk
    creamy cashew dressing 89
    creamy leek, spinach and butter bean
        bowls 183
    crispy cauliflower and thyme bake 136
    herby green sauce 77
    prep-ahead porridge 21
    seedy green pesto muffins 30
oats 24
    berry, oats and peanut butter
        smoothie 24, **25**
    carrot cake flapjacks 34
    double chocolate oaty bites 38, **39**
    freezer chocolate chip cookies 33
    oaty almond butter and apple bars 37
    prep-ahead porridge **20**, 21
    seedy green pesto muffins 30
olive, sun-dried tomato and basil pasta
    salad **80**, 81
orange 34
    chocolate orange porridge **20**, 21
orzo 175
    one-pan spinach, leek and pesto
        orzo 160, **161**
    simple tomato and basil orzo **154**, 155
    warm Mediterranean aubergine and
        basil orzo salad **48**, 49

parsley
    15-minute herby avocado noodles 82
    butter bean mash with garlicky
        almonds and greens 139
    herby green sauce 77
    herby jewelled rice with roasted
        aubergine, walnuts, mint and
        pomegranate 111
    herby summer rolls 72
    spicy sun-dried tomato and aubergine
        ragu 159
pasta
    cavolo nero and walnut spaghetti **92**,
        93
    lemony pea and broccoli pasta **124**,
        125
    my go-to green pasta **76**, 77
    one-pan spinach, leek and pesto
        orzo 160, **161**
    pan-fried sage and mushroom
        pasta 122, **123**
    roasted Mediterranean veg and
        cannellini bean tomato sauce
        179

roasted pepper, thyme and butter
bean tray bake 175
simple tomato and basil orzo **154**, 155
slow-cooked courgette, olive oil and
chilli linguine 94, **95**
spicy sun-dried tomato and aubergine
ragu **158**, 159
sun-dried tomato, basil and olive pasta
salad **80**, 81
warm Mediterranean aubergine and
basil orzo salad **48**, 49
peanut butter
berry, oats and peanut butter
smoothie 24, **25**
blueberry, banana and peanut
porridge **20**, 21
freezer chocolate chip cookies 33
harissa peanut dressing **44**, 45
one-pan peanut and cauliflower
stew 176, **177**
satay sauce 62
pea(s) 15
broccoli and walnut soup with herby
croutons 145
easy pea-sy curry 156
garlicky broccoli and chilli protein
bowls 103
green bean, spinach and cashew
curry 171
lemony pea and broccoli pasta **124**,
125
my everyday ginger and chilli stir-
fry 114
my go-to green pasta 77
one-pan spinach, leek and pesto
orzo 160
pea, lime and tahini toasts 28, **29**
pepper
10-minute miso and ginger salad 53
easy chickpea and veggie curry 167
herby summer rolls 72
roasted Mediterranean veg and
cannellini bean tomato sauce 179
roasted pepper, thyme and butter
bean tray bake **174**, 175
warm Mediterranean aubergine and
basil orzo salad 49
pesto
nourishing lentil, mushroom and pesto
soup 146, **147**
one-pan spinach, leek and pesto
orzo 160, **161**
pesto mash 130, **131**
pesto quinoa fritters 180, **181**
seedy green pesto muffins 30, **31**
pineapple 71
pitta, toasted **64**, 65
plant-based (flexitarian) approach 11
pomegranate seed 71

herby jewelled rice with roasted
aubergine, walnuts, mint and
pomegranate **110**, 111
porridge
blueberry, banana and peanut 20, 21
chocolate orange 20, 21
walnut, cinnamon and apple 20, 21
Postural Tachycardia Syndrome 10
potato
crispy potato and paprika tray
bake **120**, 121
crunchy satay potato salad 62, **63**
pesto mash 130, **131**
protein, plant-based sources 14–15
protein bowls
crunchy tofu, quinoa and tahini 104,
105
garlicky broccoli and chilli **102**, 103
pumpkin seed 24, 50, 66, 145

quinoa 15
crunchy tofu, quinoa and tahini protein
bowls 104, **105**
garlicky broccoli and chilli protein
bowls 103
mango, mint and chilli sunshine
bowls 71
my everyday ginger and chilli stir-
fry 114
pesto quinoa fritters 180, **181**
spicy black bean, quinoa and avocado
bowls 126, **127**
super green edamame salad 50
radish 104
ragu, spicy sun-dried tomato and
aubergine **158**, 159
raisin(s) 21, 34
rice
herby jewelled rice with roasted
aubergine, walnuts, mint and
pomegranate **110**, 111
miso mushroom bowls 78
one-pan peanut and cauliflower
stew 176
rice paper wrappers 72
rocket 89, 93, 111, 175

sage and mushroom pasta, pan-fried 122,
123
salads
10-minute miso and ginger salad **52**,
53
avocado and butter lettuce salad with
a crunchy protein topping 66, **67–8**
chopped guacamole-style salad 46, **47**
creamy beetroot, lentil and yoghurt
salad with toasted pitta **64**, 65
creamy tahini beans on toast 54
crunchy satay potato salad 62, **63**

garlicky barley with green bean salad
with herby almonds **132**, 133
my every single day salad **88**, 89
sun-dried tomato, basil and olive pasta
salad **80**, 81
super green edamame salad 50, **51**
warm Mediterranean aubergine and
basil orzo salad **48**, 49
salt 15
sandwiches
quick pan-fried tofu and herby yoghurt
sandwich 58, **59**
smashed chickpea guacamole
sandwich **60**, 61
satay potato salad, crunchy 62, **63**
sauces
creamy tahini 54, **55**
dipping 72, **73**
herby green **76**, 77
satay 62
tomato **178**, 179
seed(s) 15, 103
seedy green pesto muffins 30, **31**
sticky miso aubergines with crunchy
seeds **128**, 129
see also flaxseed; pumpkin seed;
sesame seed
sesame seed 78, 126
shallot, cosy roasted shallot and butter
bean bowls 98, **99**
slaw, crunchy **44**, 45
smoothies
berry, oats and peanut butter 24, **25**
sunshine mango 24, **25**
super green spinach 24, **24**
snacks 19–38
soups
chunky white bean and veggie soup
with garlic croutons **148**, 149
everyday butter bean, carrot and
sweet potato soup 142, **143**
nourishing lentil, mushroom and pesto
soup 146, **147**
pea, broccoli and walnut soup with
herby croutons **144**, 145
sourdough
avocado and butter lettuce salad with
a crunchy protein topping 66
butter beans, greens and avocado
toasts 28, **29**
creamy tahini beans on toast 54, **55**
crispy cauliflower and thyme bake
136
garlic croutons 149
harissa scrambled tofu on toast **56**,
57
herby croutons 145
mushroom, miso and tofu toasts 29,
29

sourdough (*cont.*)

    my every single day salad 89

    pea, lime and tahini toasts 28, **29**

    smashed chickpea guacamole
        sandwich 61

spaghetti, cavolo nero and walnut **92**, 93

spinach

    15-minute black dhal 85

    butter beans, greens and avocado
        toasts 28

    chunky white bean and veggie soup
        with garlic croutons 149

    comforting udon noodle bowls with
        mushroom and coconut 118

    cosy roasted shallot and butter bean
        bowls 98

    creamy beetroot, miso and tofu
        noodles 117

    creamy leek, spinach and butter bean
        bowls **182**, 183

    creamy paneer-inspired tofu 107

    green bean, spinach and cashew
        curry **170**, 171

    harissa scrambled tofu on toast 57

    herby green sauce 77

    my every single day salad 89

    my everyday ginger and chilli stir-
        fry 114

    my go-to green pasta 77

    nourishing lentil, mushroom and pesto
        soup 146

    one-pan spinach, leek and pesto
        orzo 160, **161**

    pan-fried sage and mushroom
        pasta 122

    seedy green pesto muffins 30

    spicy black bean, quinoa and avocado
        bowls 126

    super green edamame salad 50

    super green spinach smoothie 24, **24**

stews

    15-minute chickpea, edamame and
        miso 86, **87**

    creamy black bean, harissa and
        almond butter 164, **165**

    one-pan peanut and cauliflower 176,
        177

stock 15

summer rolls, herby 72, **73**

sunflower seed 30, 66, 89

supper 91–139

sweet potato

    everyday butter bean, carrot and
        sweet potato soup 142, **143**

    everyday veggie tray bake with
        mustard and cayenne pepper 134

    sweet potato and crispy lentil
        bowls with coriander and ginger
        yoghurt **96**, 97

tagine, simple veggie and apricot 168, **169**

tahini 104

    creamy tahini beans on toast 54, **55**

    crispy one-tray hispi cabbage with
        garlic yoghurt 108

    crunchy tofu, quinoa and tahini protein
        bowls 104, **105**

    miso tahini dressing 133

    pea, lime and tahini toasts 28, **29**

Tenderstem broccoli 139

teriyaki dressing 53

toasts

    butter beans, greens and avocado
        toasts 28, **29**

    creamy beetroot, lentil and yoghurt
        salad with toasted pitta **64**, 65

    creamy tahini beans on toast 54, **55**

    harissa scrambled tofu on toast **56**, 57

    mushroom, miso and tofu toasts 29,
        29

    pea, lime and tahini toasts 28, **29**

tofu 14

    15-minute herby avocado noodles 82

    comforting udon noodle bowls with
        mushroom and coconut 118

    creamy beetroot, miso and tofu
        noodles **116**, 117

    creamy paneer-inspired tofu **106**, 107

    crispy tofu goujons with pesto
        mash 130, **131**

    crunchy satay potato salad 62

    crunchy tofu, quinoa and tahini protein
        bowls 104, **105**

    harissa scrambled tofu on toast **56**, 57

    mango, mint and chilli sunshine
        bowls 71

    mushroom, miso and tofu toasts 29,
        29

    preparation 116

    quick pan-fried tofu and herby yoghurt
        sandwich 58, **59**

    roasted Mediterranean veg and
        cannellini bean tomato sauce 179

    spicy tofu bowl with crunchy slaw **44**,
        45

    sun-dried tomato, basil and olive pasta
        salad 81

tomato

    chopped guacamole-style salad 46

    chunky white bean and veggie soup
        with garlic croutons 149

    creamy paneer-inspired tofu 107

    crispy potato and paprika tray
        bake 121

    my shortcut lentil Bolognese 152

    roasted cauliflower, fennel, tomato and
        Puy lentil tray bake **162**, 163

    roasted pepper, thyme and butter
        bean tray bake 175

simple tomato and basil orzo **154**, 155

simple veggie and apricot tagine 168

spicy sun-dried tomato and aubergine
    ragu **158**, 159

sun-dried tomato, basil and olive pasta
    salad **80**, 81

tomato passata

    roasted Mediterranean veg and
        cannellini bean tomato sauce 179

    tomato sauce **178**, 179

tortilla chips (shop-bought) 46

walnuts

    cavolo nero and walnut spaghetti **92**,
        93

    herby jewelled rice with roasted
        aubergine, walnuts, mint and
        pomegranate **110**, 111

    pea, broccoli and walnut soup with
        herby croutons **144**, 145

    spicy sun-dried tomato and aubergine
        ragu 159

    sweet and spicy kale, walnut and
        chickpea salad 42, **43**

    walnut, cinnamon and apple
        porridge **20**, 21

yoghurt *see* coconut yoghurt

ACKNOWLEDGEMENTS

Every day I wake up feeling genuinely so grateful for Deliciously Ella, my role there, our community, and the knowledge that I've been lucky enough to spend over a decade doing something that I love so deeply. I know what a privilege it is to spend your career chasing a dream and seeing it slowly (with lots of backwards steps too) coming to life.

Yet, while I may have more experience than when I sat down to write my first book in 2014, I find the creative process gets more challenging each time, trying to build something that feels new, innovative and, most importantly, meaningful. Juggling writing and testing with motherhood and the day-to-day demands of the business means my time is more and more stretched, and while I may have a thousand ideas, they'd never come together in the way they have here without both our team at Deliciously Ella and the fantastic creative team who helped to bring *Healthy Made Simple* to life. It would be genuinely impossible to say thank you enough times or to emphasise just how pivotal everyone is to this process. The book may have my name on the front, but it's anything but a solo pursuit.

First and foremost, Liberty and Jo, who completely outdid themselves, testing the recipes so thoroughly and ensuring they're exactly as they should be – their creativity has been the foundation of this book. Claudie, who designed each page, bringing the vision to life. Imogen, the best editor, sounding board and support, who has brought this and the last three books together so seamlessly. Clare, for the absolutely beautiful food photos; Sophia for making the cover shoot so easy; Tamara and Charlotte for the fantastic food styling; and Hannah for the gorgeous props. The shoots were just brilliant and I'm genuinely over the moon – this is my favourite book yet.

Oli and everyone at Hodder and Yellow Kite for their ongoing support, their focus on ensuring this is the best book it can be and their desire to push our publishing as far as we can. And Cathryn, for your support – seven books later and we're still going strong!

And finally, to my family, the centre of my world: Matthew, Skye and May. None of this means anything without you.

ABOUT ELLA

Ella Mills is the founder of Deliciously Ella, a plant-based food and wellness platform, dedicated to sharing simple tools for a healthier life. She is an award-winning author and an advocate of healthy living.

Following her own experience of ill health in 2011, Ella started the popular recipe website, deliciouslyella.com, as she learnt to cook delicious, natural, plant-based food. Ever committed to helping others enjoy this approach to cooking, Ella started a series of plant-based cooking classes and supper clubs the following year. As the website grew, Ella launched a recipe app, before writing the fastest-selling debut cookbook in the UK, in early 2015. Her first book, Deliciously Ella, went on to become a *Sunday Times* number 1 bestseller, a *New York Times* bestseller and has been translated into 30 languages. She has since released a further six bestselling books that have sold over 1.5 million copies in the UK alone, and has amassed a social media audience of over 4 million people.

Ella has been working with her husband, Matthew, since shortly after the publication of her first book. Ella is the company's brand director; Matthew is the CEO. The office is based in central London, and they've grown the company to a team of 60 people. Together they have opened a restaurant, Plants, in London, where they highlight the breadth of plant-based cooking.

They have also launched multiple bestselling ranges of natural, plant-based food products, including snack bars, cereals, frozen meals, veggie burgers, pasta, sauces and soups, into over 10,000 stores across the UK. The brand is bought by millions of households in the UK and has recently launched in Ireland, Switzerland, Austria, the USA and the Netherlands.

Ella and Matthew also run a membership platform via their website, deliciouslyella.com, which has over 1,000 recipes, wellness classes and always-on members' discounts for their products.

Ella lives in London with Matthew, their daughters, Skye and May, and their dog Austin.

First published in Great Britain in 2024 by Yellow Kite
An Imprint of Hodder & Stoughton
An Hachette UK company

3

A CIP catalogue record for this title is available from the British Library

Hardback ISBN 978 1 399 71790 8
eBook ISBN 978 1 399 71789 2

Publisher: Liz Gough
Editor: Imogen Fortes
Design and art direction: Claudie Dubost
Page layout: Nicky Barneby
Food photography: Clare Winfield
Front cover and portrait photography: Sophia Spring
Food styling: Tamara Vos
Food styling assistant: Charlotte Whatcott
Prop styling: Hannah Wilkinson
Hair and make-up: Sjaniël Turrell
Senior production controller: Susan Spratt

Colour origination by Alta Image London
Printed and bound in Italy by Lego SpA

Hodder & Stoughton policy is to use papers that are natural, renewable and recyclable products and made from wood grown in sustainable forests. The logging and manufacturing processes are expected to conform to the environmental regulations of the country of origin.

Yellow Kite
Hodder & Stoughton Ltd
Carmelite House
50 Victoria Embankment
London EC4Y 0DZ

www.yellowkitebooks.co.uk
www.hodder.co.uk
www.deliciouslyella.com

Scan to add *Healthy Made Simple* recipes to your Deliciously Ella app.

Simply make sure you have the latest version of the Deliciously Ella app from the App Store or Google Play or download the Deliciously Ella app now. Scan the QR code opposite to add the recipes to your recipe library.

Not a member yet? Become a Deliciously Ella member and discover delicious ways to feel better every day with:

- 1,000+ additional plant-based recipes
- A library of 500+ exercise classes, plus hundreds of mindfulness and sleep practices
- An always-on 15% discount for our web-shop
- First access to new launches and members-only merch

You might also be interested in Ella's other bestselling books:

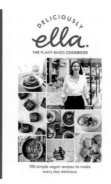
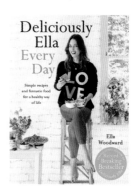

deliciouslyella.com   @deliciouslyella   @DeliciouslyElla   /DeliciouslyElla